MIDDLE EASTERN
APPROACHES

MIDDLE EASTERN APPROACHES

Experiences and Travels
of an Intelligence Officer
1939–1948

William Magan

MICHAEL RUSSELL

© W. M. T. Magan 2001

The right of W. M. T. Magan to be identified
as the author of this work has been asserted by him
in accordance with the Copyright, Designs
and Patents Act, 1988

First published in Great Britain 2001
by Michael Russell (Publishing) Ltd
Wilby Hall, Wilby, Norwich NR16 2JP

Typeset in Sabon by Waveney Typesetters
Wymondham, Norfolk
Printed and bound in Great Britain
by Biddles Ltd, Guildford and King's Lynn

ISBN 0 85955 266 7

This book is dedicated to
members of the Security Service (MI5),
men and women, past and present, who have devoted,
and are devoting, their lives anonymously to preserving
the security of the Realm.

Contents

Author's Note

I am grateful to my wife, Maxine, and to Nancy Christopherson, for their painstaking editing of the text, and to Tessa Wells for the immaculate typescript and additional editing.

Half the royalties will be given to the Security Service Benevolent Fund. MI5 have agreed to the book's publication.

I

The Mise-en-Scène

During the latter part of the summer of 1939, I was temporarily detached from my Indian Cavalry regiment, Hodson's Horse, which was serving on the North West Frontier of India, to do an intelligence familiarisation course with the Government of India's Civil Intelligence Bureau – the combined MI5 and MI6 of India – which had its headquarters in the Delhi/Simla complex.

While I was there, the Second World War broke out and, much against my will, instead of returning immediately to the command of the Mussalman Squadron of Hodson's Horse, I was ordered by the Commander-in-Chief, no less, to remain with the Intelligence Bureau as Military Liaison Officer with the Military Intelligence Directorate in Army Headquarters for six months or so, after which I would return to my regiment.

But the fates were to take command. I was never to return to my regiment. My appointment to the Intelligence Bureau was instead to lead to an Intelligence career spanning almost the next thirty years of my life, until I reached the retirement age of sixty. From the outset I found Intelligence a very engrossing, very important and very worthwhile subject, but at that time I had no intention to do other than pursue my military career as a soldier. It turned out, however, that one Intelligence job led inexorably to another and so on – jobs that I could never refuse because they were imposed upon me by the highest authorities, civil and military, with whom I could not argue, until I had become so widely experienced that Intelligence had become my second career.

Before I continue with the thread of my Intelligence career I must say something about another happening at the same time (1940) – my wonderful marriage to Maxine.

In the Delhi/Simla complex, even in wartime, there was a very active social life in which I inevitably became involved. Among the girls I came to know was Maxine Mitchell, daughter of Sir Kenneth Mitchell, a distinguished engineer. Her mother was dead. She had had the social distinction of partnering the Viceroy to open the principal ball of the season in Simla. She was the loveliest and the most intelligent of all the girls in the Delhi/Simla complex, great fun, a great doer, and very affectionate. She and I saw a lot of each other because we had many friends in common and, after she joined up for war service, we both worked in the same Intelligence department in AHQ in which she was secretary to the Director of Military Intelligence.

She got the job because when war was declared she rode the seven miles to Simla from a mountain hotel, Wildflower Hall, where she was staying, and offered her services at Army Headquarters. She was told that the HQ was adequately staffed with Indian male clerks and young ladies were not wanted. The Director of Military Intelligence, hearing of this, telephoned her and invited her to be his secretary. He knew a good candidate when he saw one.

On the outbreak of war I wrote a memorandum saying that there were a lot of very well educated girls in the Delhi/Simla complex, daughters of Indian Civil Service and Army officers, who ought to be recruited to do GIII (captains) jobs and perhaps GII (majors) jobs in Army Headquarters and to relieve officers like me to go back to our regiments to fight the war. The memorandum reached the Chief of Staff who minuted it: 'This officer is an unpractical visionary.'

I am glad to be able to relate that I lived to see women doing not only GIII and GII jobs, but also GI jobs (equivalent to lieutenant colonel's rank).

In my book *Risala, the Story of an Indian Cavalry Officer*, I recount the task I was given in 1940 of investigating the mutiny of the Sikh Squadron of the Central India Horse (CIH). It was a matter of vital interest to the higher military authorities because it might presage further disaffection among the Sikhs in the Indian Army.

The mutiny took place in Bombay harbour where the regiment was waiting to embark for the Middle East. It was Communist inspired. The regiment had been stationed in Meerut where the Indian Communist Party had its head-quarters. One man in the regiment, Bishan Singh, had been suborned and fully indoctrinated by the Communists. The regiment was moving to the Middle East but was delayed for two days in Bombay docks by bad weather.

Europe had just been overrun by Hitler and the Italians had entered the war as allies of Germany and were threatening the Middle East and East Africa. In accordance with the left wing dissident propaganda line Bishan Singh put the following proposition to the CIH Sikh squadron:

The British, now alone, cannot survive against Germany and Italy and will be overrun by them. British rule in India will collapse. In that case, the greatly preponderant Muslim pop-ulation in the Punjab will try to overrun the Sikhs. The right place for Sikh soldiers, therefore, is at home in the Punjab, guarding their wives and families, and not fighting Britain's inevitably losing battle against more powerful European enemies in Egypt.

The unfortunate squadron fell for the bait and mutinied.

The whole squadron was sent back under arrest to Bolarum in the south of India where they had been stationed. It was 1,500 miles from Simla where the Director of Military Intelligence, to whom I had to report, had his office. He sent my reports to the Commander-in-Chief, and Maxine was given the task of taking them to him.

I have always thought that if you want to be listened to, your reports must be interesting, and Maxine says that her interest in me was aroused by my first report, which she started to read on her way to the Commander-in-Chief's office. She says it started like this: 'Bishan Singh sat slumped in his chair in the middle of the cell under a bare electric light bulb.'

She found that such a startling change from normal formal intelligence reports that she withdrew to the ladies' lavatory and read the whole report, and did so thereafter with my subsequent reports.

A year after we had first got to know each other, the best thing that has ever happened to me in life occurred when we got engaged. After sixty years of marriage, she is still as lovely, lively, intelligent, amusing and affectionate as ever, and as energetic a doer as she always was.

We were married at the Church of the Redemption, New Delhi, by the Bishop of Lahore. In the office, the evening before our wedding, I asked Ross Howman, who shared the room with me, whether he had a car at the office. He had, and asked why I wanted to know. 'Because', I said, 'I would like you to take me to the chemist in Connaught Place [the main Delhi shopping area] to get some medicine. I'm not well.'

'Oh,' he said, 'I felt like that the evening before I got married.' At all events, he took me, and I got the quinine I needed as I had a bad relapse of malaria. I was married next day with a temperature of 103°, and spent the following couple of days ill in bed.

My regiment had by then been moved from Loralai on the Frontier to Meerut, only forty miles from Delhi, and they did us proud. They sent a guard of honour, and Maxine and I left the church under an arch of crossed lances.

I think we got a week's leave, which we spent in Kulu. We had lovely walks, some of them in the snow – which had come low down on the mountains – and Maxine painted watercolours. She started me off on a holiday painting career which has ever since been a recurring pleasure and interest to us both, because our holidays are, whenever we can manage it, joint painting holidays.

I had twice descended from the stark world of the high

Himalayas into the Kulu valley, and it had seemed a paradise on earth. And it still seemed so on our honeymoon, but this time it was winter. Instead of tents, we rented a very small house. It was little more than a stone hut. Downstairs there was a small living-room of sorts, and some cooking arrangements. Upstairs was one bedroom with 'bathroom' off it. The bathroom stood out from the main structure of the hut so that when you were bathing you could see through the wide cracks in the floor boards the snow below, and the icicles hanging under the eaves. The bath was a zinc tub for which we had to carry kerosene cans of hot water upstairs.

Compared with the high Himalayas, this would have seemed palatial, but it was rather below the standard of comfort to which Maxine was accustomed. However, she took it all in good part.

Our first married home was in what was known as 'tented accommodation' in a tented camp on the outskirts of New Delhi. Those who had served in India had known for a very long time how to make themselves comfortable in tents. We had three large tents which were joined together: one was the sitting-room, a second the dining-room, and the third our bedroom. There was a smaller bath tent with the usual Indian zinc bath tub and 'other conveniences', and there was a small kitchen tent, and a servants' tent.

To have got married in November 1940, only a few months after Hitler had extinguished the lights all over Europe, now looks scarcely prudent. We had the prospect of a long war ahead of us which many of us in the armed forces were clearly not going to survive. Anyway, we did it and were in the event fortunate. We had our moment of domestic bliss before the ensuing wartime disruption of our family life.

In June 1941 Germany invaded Russia; that was a direct land threat to India. If the Germans could capture south Russia, they could break through the Caucasus, and the way would be open to them to invade India through Persia. The Shah of Persia had committed himself heavily towards the

Germans. Persia was swarming with German advisers, technicians and so on, some of whom had under-cover clandestine roles. To neutralise that potentially dangerous situation, therefore, British and Indian forces from India occupied Iraq and parts of west Persia, and claimed the right to operate in south and east Persia. The Russians, likewise, occupied north Persia. The old Shah, Reza Khan, abdicated and was exiled to South Africa, where he died.

The other major development was that in December 1941 the Japanese attacked the American naval Pacific base, Pearl Harbor, bringing both themselves and the Americans into the war. Simultaneously they began an astounding assault on South East Asia. By the end of January 1942 they had occupied all of Malaya – which was British colonial territory. India was thus threatened from the east as well as from the west. We in India now had the war on our doorstep.

In January 1942 I was invited by Sir Dennis Pilditch, Director of the Indian Intelligence Bureau, to go and have a word with him at his private residence. He said that, as I would be well aware, the Japanese had unexpectedly overrun Malaya from the north, and no advance intelligence preparations had been made to deal with such a situation. We had no 'stay behind' organisation to provide us with intelligence from behind the Japanese lines or to commit sabotage there. If the commander-in-chief of the German forces in south Russia, Field-Marshal von Bock, was to succeed in breaking through the Caucasus into Persia as a prelude to attacking India we did not want to be caught in a similar situation there. He said he was speaking with the full knowledge and authority of the Commander-in-Chief, India, and was going to put a proposition to me with which the Commander-in-Chief was in full agreement.

He then asked me if I, as a Persian speaker and having knowledge of the country from having lived there for a year, would go into south and east Persia and try to form a 'stay behind' organisation to provide intelligence from behind the German lines in Persia if they succeeded in getting there. He went on to say that the Germans had left their own 'stay behind' organisation in Persia which had gone underground. PAIFORCE (Persia and Iraq Force) which had its headquarters in Baghdad in Iraq, was trying to mop that up.

A promising double agent case, known as the Silver case, had been initiated by the Intelligence Bureau who were using it to send false information to the German Legation in Kabul. He would like me to study the possibility of having a link of the case to Berlin through the Middle East, to which end I was to liaise with those working on DA (double agent) cases from Persia and the Middle East.

Silver came from the North West Province of India, bordering on Afghanistan. He was a member of the Indian Communist Party and actively anti-British. He spoke Hindustani, Pashtu, English and Afghani Persian.

When India declared war on Germany in 1939 Silver thought that the best way in which he could damage the British was to give information about British India to the German legation in Kabul, the capital of Afghanistan. He had no access to information of any importance. He went to Kabul with such information as he had. On his return he was arrested and imprisoned.

When Germany declared war on Russia in 1941, it meant that the British and Communist Russia were allies against the Germans. We therefore asked Silver whether he would be prepared to work for us and the Russians against the Germans. He agreed.

We therefore sent Silver back to the German legation in Kabul. He was to tell the Germans that he was now working for an anti-British organisation with widespread contacts throughout India which could supply unlimited information, but it would be very expensive as it would cost his organisation a lot of money to gather the information. He took a long written report with him and demanded a large sum for it. It contained a lot of true and factual information of no importance, on which the Germans could check, and some very important

[17]

and misleading information. We kept the Russians informed of what we were doing and Silver gave their legation in Kabul a copy of the report.

Having sent Silver to Kabul several times with such reports, and having taken all the gold that they had off the German legation, we told Silver to tell the Germans that his anti-British organisation had a trained signaller who would work from Delhi if a wireless link was arranged between Kabul and India. That was done and the wireless link worked.

It was then suggested to the German legation in Kabul that there should be a direct wireless link to the German Intelligence headquarters in Berlin, and that was arranged. From then on we had three wireless schedules daily to Berlin from our hide-out in the Viceroy's garden in Delhi, on which we sent a mass of false and misleading information. For the sake of notional security we kept changing the times of the schedules, but there was always one in the middle of the night and our wives wondered what we were doing when we got up at two or three o'clock in the morning and went out to some undisclosed place on some undisclosed mission.

I ran the Silver case together with my Indian Police colleague the late Malcolm Johnston. We attended every wireless schedule to the Germans so that we could answer any difficult questions that might be asked. Our communications with the Germans were in English, and in the Morse code. Our signaller was Corporal Lappin of the Royal Corps of Signals, a very discreet, likeable and efficient technician.

The two main purposes of this operation were first to put across false order of battle information, and secondly for counter-intelligence purposes. We could provide what to the enemy would seem to be a safe rendezvous to which to send any other agents whom they might wish to despatch.

The Germans passed our information to the Japanese, so our reports were larded with false information to mislead the Japanese in Burma and the Far East. The Japanese sent a party of Indian wireless agents from Burma who landed in Madras.

We caught them and persuaded two of them to work for us, so we also then had a direct wireless link to the Japanese Military Headquarters in Rangoon. They also sent a second batch of Indian wireless agents. We undertook to provide, in the eyes of the Japanese, a safe rendezvous for them and rounded them up when they landed.

Eventually, for whatever reason, the Russians told the Germans that the Silver case was a British hoax. The Germans did not believe them and carried on with the case. Subhas Chandra Bose, the well-known Indian revolutionary leader, who was with the Germans in Berlin, also expressed doubts about it, but the Germans took no notice of him.

Ever since I had become involved in Intelligence I had been trying, as I have said, to get back to my regiment where I was the commander of a squadron of Indian Cavalry – no better job in the world at my then time of life – and although I was still rather forlornly hoping to do so, I clearly could not refuse this request to carry out the Persian operation. The invitation was in effect a polite way of giving me an order endorsed by the Commander-in-Chief. Also it made very good sense that some-one should attempt to do what was required, and I was the only person with both Persian knowledge and experience and the required relationship with the Intelligence organisation in India, to whom I would be reporting.

Moreover, knowing, as I did, the long history of India, I was conscious that a threat from the west once again faced her by the historic invasion route through the passes of the North West Frontier, and it was thus perhaps appropriate that I, who had first served in the 12th Cavalry (Sam Browne's), an old Punjab Frontier Force regiment, whose raison d'être it was to guard that region, was being sent to make what contribution I could to forestalling this new threat to the area.

The Government of India Intelligence Bureau, to which I would be reporting, had a local office at Quetta on the North West Frontier, which was to be my local base in India. It was also on my route into Persia.

From my experience of Persia, I knew that my prime need would be efficient transport. There were in those days no modern roads in Persia, only tracks, terribly rough, pot-holed and corrugated. A fairly powerful sturdy vehicle was therefore an essential need. It was before the days of four-wheel drive vehicles such as Land Rovers, so I had to make do as best I could with a not sturdy enough motor-car. That, and various other arrangements, settled, I set off for Persia overland through Baluchistan, where I stopped for a few days in Quetta, the last major town in India before the long drive over an awful dusty track to the Persian border. In Quetta I established a support base for myself and my coming operations with the Quetta Intelligence Bureau. It was also clear to me that I must have a Persian-speaking driver; someone who could at least guard the car, and help to dig it out when, as would be inevitable at times in the Persian deserts, we would get stuck in soft sand.

The Quetta Bureau managed to borrow from the Quetta Police a police sergeant, a Hazara bilingual in Persian and Hindustani. He and I used both languages indiscriminately when talking to each other. He was happy to come with me, and to face whatever was in store for us. As a police officer, he knew how to be wholly discreet. His name was Ibrahim Khan. Ibrahim is pronounced 'ee-BRAI-heem'. The middle syllable is strongly accented. He proved to be not only an excellent man, but a very nice one with whom I felt wholly at ease. It was one of those cases where the chemistry of friendship was entirely right, and we became very firm friends, motoring many thousands of dusty miles together as we flogged through the enormous distances of desert, wilderness and mountains that are Persia, often living and sleeping rough, perhaps on the ground, wrapped in a blanket, and eating rough in Persian *chai-kahnehs* – little tea stalls. He had been in the armed forces in the First World War and, far from having any grumbles about the life we were leading, said how lucky we were to have a motor vehicle – even one that gave us endless trouble. 'Last time', he said, 'we had to do it on our flat feet.'

I needed two bases in Persia, one in the south east, the other in Teheran where I could liaise with PAIFORCE. I chose Kerman as my south east Persia base, where I arranged to be nominally attached to the British Consulate as a temporary military vice-consul engaged rather vaguely on 'road and other reconnaissance'. The consulate was manned by a member of the Indian Foreign and Political Service, with a vice-consul from the same service.

It was essential that I should have some credible cover for my covert operation, otherwise I would stand out like a sore thumb. Our Sappers were repairing the roads to enable our forces to move into Persia from India if necessary. I, as someone with a knowledge of Persia, and as a Persian interpreter, made a credible adviser to the Sappers and liaison officer for them with the Persian authorities, and general reconnaissance officer making advance preparation for the arrival of our forces. This cover I judged to be enough to account for the widespread travelling I would have to do throughout the enormous area of south, central and east Persia.

2

Persia

With everything settled in Quetta, Ibrahim and I set off into the Persian wilds. I was the only British military officer in that immense wilderness and desert area of southern, central and eastern Persia, except for the few Sappers who were working to improve the roads.

Once across the frontier into Persia, I began to plan and execute my tasks in detail. I think my considerable Himalayan experience of making do somehow in vast areas of desolation was useful, in that I felt no qualms at being able to compete with whatever difficulties might arise. I was careful to do nothing to cause antipathy to me, or my presence, among the Persians. I cultivated my contacts with care, and not least people of influence. I became very friendly with both the Persian general commanding the Persian forces in south east Persia, whose headquarters were in Kerman, and with the local chief of police. I used to visit them in their offices when I was in Kerman to make them feel assured that I was doing nothing that could damage Persian interests. They knew that my ostensible task was route reconnaissance and liaison officer for the Sappers (who, themselves, did not know the real raison d'être for my presence in the area), and that this necessitated endless travel. I made it clear that, being closely associated with the British Sappers who were working to improve the roads, which would benefit everyone locally, I could, if the general or police chief wanted any particular road construction carried out, convey their wishes to the Chief Royal Engineer. These senior Persians were intelligent men of the world and did nothing to obstruct me. Indeed other Persians told me that they welcomed our presence. South and east Persia had a very close association with

British India and, in particular, strong and important trade links, and they were horrified at the thought of coming under the heel of Hitler's Germany. In consequence the area as a whole was well disposed towards the British and welcomed our interest in frustrating the German advance there.

To establish my pied-à-terre in Teheran I contacted the small PAIFORCE Security Intelligence organisation there – five officers and two NCOs, all 'civilians in uniform', having joined the forces for the war. They appeared to have been hand-picked, as they were a very gifted lot of people and included some Persian speakers. Attached to them, mainly for guard duties, were two or three Polish soldiers who had evaded the German forces, and made their way across Russia to Persia.

The little unit had various defence functions concerned with the prosecution of the war, not least of which was mopping up the 'stay-behind' Germans and neutralising their collaborators, at which they were having notable successes. The officers consisted of an engineer, a stockbroker, a schoolmaster, an Englishman who had formerly been a Russian Army officer, and a university don. The two NCOs consisted of a university don who was fluent in Persian, and an Englishman who had been brought up in Persia and was also fluent in the language.

The stockbroker was Alan Roger. While I was in Delhi he came out to India on an economics mission with his father, Sir Alexander Roger, a distinguished businessman. Alan had been turned down for an Army commission in Britain on health grounds. He took the opportunity while in India to apply again. The Indian authorities accepted him and gave him a commission in the Indian Army. He was posted to my office in Delhi and came to live with Maxine and me and her father as he had no accommodation. He was so able that I recommended him to PAIFORCE who were very short of good Intelligence officers. PAIFORCE posted him to Teheran to open up their Security Intelligence office there. He was to become a lifelong friend of Maxine's and mine.

As the only regular service officer, I resolved to give them all the help I could with the quasi-military operations when I could make time. Mopping up the well-concealed Germans was not a task for conventional military forces. It was a rat-catching operation, and our little group were the rat-catchers, a role I myself was very ready to assume.

However, it was clear to me that during the first six months or so that I was in Persia, I would have to devote myself unremittingly to what I had to do in central, east and south Persia to prepare for a German break through the Caucasus. As I saw the situation when I was given the assignment, the Germans, in January 1942, were bogged down in south Russia by the winter, but would be on the move again when the spring thaw came and might, by my calculations, get through the Caucasus by the early autumn of 1942. I had, therefore, perhaps six to eight months to complete my task. It was going to be hard going, and I worked seven days a week throughout much of that period, travelling thousands of hard and dusty miles.

But there was another side to my life. I had left a young wife and child in India, and I wrote to her often and fully. I could not, of course, say anything about my official assignments, but I could and did describe my daily life in Persia, a good deal of it out of the ordinary and interesting. Maxine kept all my letters and I draw on them extensively in what follows.

The operations on which I was engaged consisted of finding and recruiting suitable agents – that was up to me. Training them in what they would have to do and how to do it – that was up to the support operation in India. Finding safe cover for their operations – that too was up to me. And this work had to be done in such a covert way that no one should detect that it was happening.

I was not involved in the agents' training, but they were to use wireless and, when they could safely do so, to slip across the border into Quetta to be debriefed. The information that was wanted was the size of enemy forces, the identity of units, including artillery, if possible, and the numbers and type of armoured vehicles.

We decided against sabotage agents. There was no railway in eastern Persia, really nothing to sabotage on the desert roads, no important bridges for instance, and we were not prepared to risk losing agents on sabotage operations against the German forces.

It was essential that I should not expose myself by personally trying to recruit agents, but here I had a good start. An American, I will call him Robert Peel, who had a carpet business in Persia, made a business trip to Delhi, and when he was there made contact with the Intelligence Bureau, which was an overt organisation with its name in the telephone directory, and offered his services if he could be any use. He had his headquarters in Isfahan in Persia.

When I visited Quetta on my way into Persia he was summoned there to meet me. There was no problem about that because he visited Quetta from time to time on business.

The head of the Quetta Intelligence Bureau saw him and outlined what was required and asked him whether he would be prepared to participate in my operation. He agreed enthusiastically. He was then introduced to me and we had a long talk. We could only talk generalities at that stage, but we were agreed that the most likely way of finding suitable agents was through the carpet industry, a good deal of which was in the hands of Europeans, many of whom were known to Peel. Most of them were Greeks who were thoroughly anti-German (because the Germans had brutally overrun Greece a year earlier) and would therefore, be likely to agree to work for us if we thought they were suitable.

When we discussed how recruited agents could be got to India for training we thought the best plan would be to smuggle them if necessary through Zahidan, the frontier town between Persia and India. If possible they would go on their own and be met in Baluchistan by an Indian Persian-speaking officer of the Quetta Intelligence Bureau or they could be taken to Zahidan and handed over there. There were at all times quite a large number of people travelling between India and

Persia through Zahidan so the movement of our agent would not stand out as anything unusual. I think it was an open frontier, but if documents were needed we would have had no difficulty in supplying them.

In addition to Peel I had two other helpers. The Government of India agreed to open a vice-consulate at Yezd in central Persia and to appoint a Persian-speaking Indian from the Indian Police as vice-consul. This was a clearly a sensible appointment because Yezd is largely a Zoroastrian town, Parsees with strong links with the large Parsee community in India.

My other helper was a Greek carpet merchant whom I had got to know when I spent a year in Persia on Persian study leave. I knew him exceedingly well and believed him to be wholly discreet. He had his main business in Kerman.

I needed to meet my assistants often and to do so clandestinely, and that was far from easy. We did so by arranging, whenever we met, some pre-arranged place and date for the next meeting. I had to guide them in detail both as to the suitability of people they proposed to contact and recruit and their location for carrying out their task if the Germans got as far.

I insisted that no potential agent was to be approached without my explicit permission. I also insisted that nothing was to be recorded on paper which could reveal details of the operation. We also wrote no letters. All communication must be oral, which was one reason for the immense amount of travelling I had to do, because I also insisted on visiting my subordinates rather than them visiting me. To have a succession of people, two of them in the carpet trade, calling on me might raise suspicions. I did not meet any of the agents we recruited, and none of them ever knew of my existence. We divided up the country territorially between my three subordinates – the American, the Indian police officer, and my Greek carpet-seller. All of this involved an immense amount of very detailed and difficult work which had to be done in complete secrecy and with great urgency. All of it paid off and by the end of six moths we had nine trained agents strategically placed on the routes through Persia to India. There are only two main routes, one through central Persia, the other through north Persia, with another two possibles, one through the great central desert, the other mostly by sea through the Persian Gulf.

The agents were very well rewarded by the Government of India and were promised large bonuses if it came to working behind German lines.

Now let us travel the Persian roads.

3
The End of the Beginning

The awful pounding that my motor-car received started as soon as Ibrahim and I left Quetta for Zahidan (the Persian frontier town en route for Kerman) – a total journey of some 450 miles. I wrote of

> the long and dusty drive across Baluchistan parallel to the single track railway line to the terminal in Persia at the frontier town of Zahidan – a one-horse little place – that took two days, during which we had at times to dig ourselves out of the soft sand – we soon became experts at dealing with sand.

I had taken the precaution to bring with me sand mats and shovels, strapped to the bonnet of the car. The sand mats were strong canvas cane-reinforced strips which could be laid on the surface of the sand for the wheels of the car to run over.

From Zahidan we set out for Kerman, a drive of 300 miles of very rough going which involves crossing the Lut Desert, always somewhat hazardous on account of heat and aridity, and of one substantial area of treacherous soft sand known as the Shor-Guz. The Persians said that you could not survive in the desert for more than two hours without water in the daytime in summer. I crossed that desert many times and got to know it very well, and indeed developed a strong love/hate relationship with it. In the midst of it was like being at sea. There it was no longer possible to see the surrounding mountain ranges and I used to think of it as being 'out of sight of land'. On the western verge of the desert are the remains of an ancient 'light-house' erected centuries ago by a caring and understanding Persian monarch to guide caravans crossing the desert in the cool of the night.

Once off the desert to the west, the track climbs through the foothills towards the central Persian plateau, and soon passes the amazing deserted mud-brick city of Bam. The track then winds on through a beautiful wilderness of mountains, and finally tops a ridge some twenty miles from Kerman at Persia's loveliest village, Mahan.

The beauty of Mahan derives in large degree from the stark contrasts of the scene. The village lies in a wholly barren, rough gravelly plain. The backdrop to that is an enormous snow mountain immediately behind the village rising to 15,000 feet – the Koo-i-Jupa. It is a village of customary small tawny dwellings, but streams from the mountain enable cypress and other trees to provide a contrasting screen of greenery. And crowning the rustic village dwellings is a fine blue-domed mosque, and four unusually elegant and distinguished minarets, also blue-tiled – a pair at each end of the village. It is hardly possible to describe its ethereal beauty.

From there a switchback drive along the skirt of the mountains leads to the small mud-brick town of Kerman, situated on the plateau some 6,000 feet above sea level. There Tony Clinton-Thomas, the Vice-Consul at the British Indian Consulate, kindly let me have a room in his house, and another in his servants' quarters as a pied-à-terre for myself and Ibrahim, whenever we should be in Kerman.

I did not linger long in Kerman. I had reckoned that the first thing I must do was to reconnoitre the whole area, looking at it from the German point of view. What would they do if they got there? What therefore should I do to frustrate them? It meant a lot of hard driving and hard work.

I knew the history of this enormous area of desert and wilderness – one of the most inhospitable places on earth and, in particular, a destroyer of armies. The fabulous Queen Semiramis of Babylon (ninth century BC) and Cyrus the Great of

Persia (sixth century BC) took their armies through it and, in each case, only a handful of men survived. Alexander the Great (fourth century BC) suffered a similar disaster on his return march from India. He is said to have lost 25,000 men in the southern part of this desert area; some accounts put the figure as high as 40,000.

I was going to have to spend the next six months, and perhaps more, in this vast rugged, arid region, and my operations were conditioned by my judgement that it would still prove a hazardous place even for modern armies, as the Germans would discover. And, like Alexander the Great more than 2,000 years earlier, I chose Kerman as the best centre for control of operations throughout the whole of the eastern and southern Persian deserts.

Because of the enormous area in which I had to operate, and the awful condition of the roads and tracks, my motor vehicle, an ordinary touring car, was soon wearing out. To borrow something sturdier from the Army would have made me too conspicuous. I needed to travel fast and to travel far. After some months Ibrahim, too, an older man than I, was feeling the strain. Here is part of my description of a typical journey. I was in Teheran in mid-May 1942 and needed to get quickly to Zahidan, 1,100 miles away along the awful roads, for consultation there with my support group from Quetta. I wrote this on the writing pad I always carried on my travels:

… I am sitting in the middle of the desert with a broken steering gear hoping that some other vehicle will pass this way today. The roads are so absolutely hellish that it is impossible to keep a car together, and the trouble is that it is two or three hundred miles between towns, and it is in many places not wise to be out at night, so one has to rattle along to make the distance in the day.

As I was writing this, Ibrahim sighted a sail so we hoisted our shirt. When it came alongside, it turned out to be what is known here as an *auto-boose*. I got a seat in it as far as Yezd.

There I found a mechanic and took him in a hired car to where my car was. We took off the broken bit of the steering gear and returned with it to Yezd where he welded it together. We then took it back and fitted it on the car. It was by then 7 o'clock in the evening. Everything seemed to fit all right, so we started once more.

We drove all through the night and reached Kerman at 6 a.m. I decided to start again from there at noon, and had hoped to get in a couple of hours' sleep. However I was so busy that I got no sleep and did not get off till late. We reached Bam, near the edge of the Lut desert, at about 6.30 p.m. It is now too hot to cross the desert by day so I decided to do as much of it as I could that night.

I had some supper at Bam with a very nice Swiss engineer who is working on the desert road, and he gave me a guide, an extraordinary wild Arab, who spoke both Hindustani and Persian. We started again at 10 o'clock at night. Poor Ibrahim was very tired and slept somehow or other in the back of the car in great discomfort. He was too tired to drive so the Arab and I took it in turns. We stuck for two hours in the sand in one place, but, although it was night, managed to get some men working on the desert road to dig us out. Ibrahim managed somehow to sleep through the whole operation. Eventually at 3.30 a.m. we reached a place where we could get no further until daylight on account of a bad patch of soft sand. There was a small Persian police post there – a much worse and hotter place than anything P.C. Wren ever imagined for the Foreign Legion. We lay down in the sand to sleep for an hour. A sleep broken by flies and gnats and the groans of a poor devil who I think was dying.

At 4.30 a.m. we were off again. We were nearly two hours crossing the next mile of sand, and then got onto better going. We then shed the Arab guide. We had a frightfully hot drive on, with a following wind all the way and got to Zahidan about 3 o'clock in the afternoon. I had had only one broken hour's sleep in the previous sixty hours.

Towards the end of July 1942, I returned to India for conferences. I wrote to Maxine:

> I am greatly looking forward to seeing you again in a few days, dearest, and Thomas, and the dogs (excuse them in the same sentence, but they are all part of the family). I wonder if there is any news of Sprag.

Sprag Mitchell was Maxine's brother, a most attractive, light-hearted, joyous young man, who had come out to India in the summer of 1939 from Christ Church, Oxford, for part of the 'long vac', to be with her and their father. He was still in India when the war broke out. He immediately applied to join the forces, and was commissioned into the Gunners. In the summer of 1942 he was reported missing in the Western Desert in Egypt.

I decided that when I was in India I would get rid of my car. It was falling to pieces and giving endless trouble and I was in constant anxiety that it would let me down at a crucial moment. I needed something tougher to stand up to the Persian roads and, in Quetta, on my way back to Simla, I managed to get a sturdy Chevrolet truck chassis and engine, and arranged for an Indian carpenter to make a solid station-wagon type body for it while I was in Simla.

After my conferences in Simla I was delayed getting back to Quetta by exceptional floods in the Indus. It had washed away its banks and the railway line, and was said to be thirteen miles wide in one place.

Back in Quetta:

> I have been staying here with the Keens. They have been very kind to me, but I am moving today into the dak bungalow. Butter, food, coal, etc., are very hard to come by, and I don't like to think I am consuming their rations.
>
> I have my new car. I have had all the springs strengthened. I now feel I shall travel in mental comfort, and shall be able to take all the kit and water which I may want.

Someone has been paying you compliments. Mrs Keen told me that some woman at a Red Cross party yesterday morning told her that you are very beautiful – blonde – and equally nice, which she said was a high compliment from a woman. I said that, as far as I could remember, you are not blonde – are you?

En route back to Persia I wrote:

Here I am writing to you again from Dalbandin, from where I wrote you a letter last March. I left Quetta this morning a little after 6.30 a.m. and got here – some 220 miles – comfortably for tea. We were a little later starting than I had meant to be but that is always the way on the first day on a new journey with new equipment – this time the new car. Items of kit don't quite know where they ought most conveniently to pack themselves; ropes, straps and pieces of wire have not yet discovered what they can best do. The second day their experience enables them to do better; the third all are properly assembled; the ropes are pulling their weight, and the packing and unpacking, which took an hour with difficulty the first day, completes itself in fifteen minutes.

We have been having a good journey. The car, with its additional room, good springs, powerful engine and large wheels is splendid and, *inshallah*, I am going to travel with ease and without worry. We have had no trouble at all, and have come easily through places where I would have stuck in the old car.

At a later date:

The car continues to do fine. The body, being rough carpenter made, is falling off, but we can keep hammering nails into it, and I don't care so long as the chassis, engine and springs remain good.

More agreeable than a running commentary on the performance of the vehicle were references to our baby Thomas's coming first birthday: 'This brings you and Thomas many happy returns of his birthday. Tell him I am very pleased with him, and with his mother.'

At first I had concentrated my attention on the southern and south eastern part of my area, Zahidan, Kerman, Yezd and Isfahan. I then had to go to Meshed, the most north easterly town of any size in Persia.

From Teheran:

I have been exceedingly busy here for the past two days, and am off at crack of dawn to Meshed.

I have had a very successful time. I find the people very sensible, level-headed and helpful. The near approach of the Germans has made everything much more interesting. Facts and realities become clearer, and it is easier to see what course to steer.

Tonight I am meeting General Quinan, the commander of PAIFORCE, who wants a talk with me.

In Teheran, I had to coordinate my plans with those of PAIFORCE, and also keep the British Legation fully informed of my plans and undertakings. I also had to make foolproof arrangements to pass through the Russian zone to Meshed. I was going there to see how my plans for stay behind agents in East Persia were getting on.

The journey from Teheran to Meshed took me through the Russian-occupied area of Persia, and I turned myself into a British official mail courier so as to have unassailable credentials. It is 600 miles and took two days. The little town of Shahrud is about half way, and I spent the night there. Let me give the description I wrote at the time of the night in Shahrud as being typical both of a night in a small north Persian inn, and of an encounter with the Russians:

I stopped the night at a little pub, a replica, I imagine, of a thousand other little pubs between this and Moscow. A little door led in from the street and, behind windows stocked with bottles of vodka, wines and beer, was the parlour, a bare room furnished with bare wooden benches and tables spread with Persian carpets. In one corner was a wireless. Across the passage was the kitchen where servants in their shirt-sleeves were busy at a huge oven under which blazed a fire of logs. Two or three men with no apparent purpose sat about in the kitchen smoking their long *chapooks* and drinking tea out of little glasses known as *finjans*. Behind, and down a few steps, was an open bricked courtyard with tables and chairs for guests, and some flower beds. And inside the house, up a short flight of steps, were three guest rooms leading off a passage, the last of which was assigned to me.

I was so covered with fine dust that I looked like a miller. There were no washing facilities in the pub, so I took an escort, a bootblack, who plied his trade outside the door of the pub, and was ready to earn a few krans any way he could, and went to the local *hamam*, or public bath. It was a noisome place, but I got a cubicle to myself with a shower in it. There were two taps labelled 'hot' and 'cold', but both produced rather smelly scalding water, and I managed with some difficulty to clean myself, listening as I did so to the slappings and gurglings of the faithful enjoying to the full all the delights to which the Persian bath attendant subjects his customers. There was also in my cubicle an elegant and almost poetical notice written with that economy of language which so distinguishes the best Persian style, and in a calligraphy which was truly artistic, telling customers to be careful of their valuables for the management could take no responsibility for losses. It was so brief and striking that I committed it to memory.

While I was supping off a tender chicken, a bowl of greasy soup and some salad, the man of all works, corresponding to the 'butler' in an Irish hotel, came in and said, 'Berlin is finished. Wiped off the map.' 'That's good,' I replied; 'Who managed that feat?' 'The Russians. It's completely wiped from the face of the earth. What's more, the Germans are in full retreat.' 'Splendid!' I said, 'Where are they retreating?' 'All along the whole front' was his reply. 'The Germans are utterly finished.' He had got the news, he said, from a friend who had heard it on the wireless. So, with those comforting tidings, I picked the bones of my chicken dry, leaving just enough to interest the half dozen or so cats which had appeared through the window and had been mobbing me ever since my supper had arrived.

After supper, I sat in the courtyard for a bit in the cool fresh air of the evening, and then went to bed. I slept for a little, but a swarm of sandflies, and the ever-increasing noise in the bar as the guests grew merrier, and the blaring of oriental music on the wireless, soon had me awake again. At about half-past eleven there came a knocking on my door. I said nothing, as I thought it might be another guest wanting to share my room, and I hoped he would get sick of knocking and go away. But the knocking grew more persistent, so I shouted in a sleepy voice, 'Go away. What do you want?' The man of all works replied, 'The Russians have come, and they want to see your passport.' I said, 'Tell them that this is no time of night to come waking me up, so they can go away and come back in the morning.' There was some mumbling, and then the voice again began, 'They say they must see your passport now, and also that you must move your car out of the street.' 'Tell them that I am a British officer, and they can see my papers in the morning, and that I am damned if I am going to move my car, as it is not in anyone's way and I have to start early in the morning.' There was more mumbling, and then, 'They say they must see your papers and they won't go away till they have done so.' 'Very well then, bring them in.' 'But I can't get in. I've been trying for the last ten minutes and the door is locked.' 'It isn't locked, you ass. Open it!'

He opened it and came in followed by two Russians. The officer was a nice clean-looking little man with a long, sad moustache. His orderly was a huge man with a Mongoloid face. They both saluted, and I sat up in bed

The officer talked to the waiter in Russian, and he translated into Persian.

'He says, who are you?'

'Tell him that I am a British officer coming from the British Legation in Teheran and carrying official mail for the British Consul-General in Meshed.'

Some mumbling in Russian. The Russian officer took out his notebook. 'He says, what's your name?' I gave it and the Russian wrote it down. More mumbling. 'He wants to know the name of your family.'

'That is the name of my family.'

More mumbling. 'He wants to know what your own name is.'

'That is my own name, and the name of my family.'

A lot of mumbling and head-shaking. However they seemed to manage to resolve this difficulty.

'He wants to know your rank.'

'*Sargurd, yawar*, major in English.'

'Ah!' said the Russian officer, '*capataine*!'

'No,' I said, 'try one higher', making the appropriate gesture of pointing upwards.

'Ah!' he said again. '*Maiyor*.'

'*Ji. Han. Yar. Balli*,' I said, making various noises of assent. 'Quite right.' He wrote it down. More mumbling.

'He says he wants to see your passport.'

'Tell him I haven't got one,' I replied, being as obtuse as I could.

'He says he is going to the Commandant to tell him that you refuse to show him your passport.'

'Tell him that I haven't got one, but if he wants further proof of what I say he can look at the seals on the official mail bag, and can also see my special pass from the Government of India.'

The officer then examined the seals and labels on the mail bag, taking at least five minutes over it.

'He says he can't read it.'

[37]

'Of course he can't. It's written in English.'

'He says, if it had been written in Russian he could read it. Now he says he's going to tell the Commandant that you won't show him your papers.'

'Tell him I have offered to show him my special pass from the Government of India.'

'He says he would like to see it.'

I got it out and showed it to him. The orderly joined in the long scrutiny.

'He says it ought to be written in Russian because he can't read it.'

'Tell him that I am very sorry but the Indian Government does not conduct its business in Russian.'

'He says you ought to have got a translation in Russian from the Russian Legation in Teheran.'

'Tell him that I inquired about this in Teheran, and was told that as I was carrying official mail no special pass was necessary.'

There was then a lot of head-shaking and mumbling.

'He says that he apologises very sincerely for waking you up at this time of night, but that it is his duty and that his duty had to come before all other considerations.'

'That is perfectly all right, and I quite understand it.'

'He says he would like to say how sorry he is, but that he had no alternative but to do his duty.'

'Tell him that I quite understand.'

'He says that he did not mean to inconvenience you, but that he had to comply with his orders and that his duty ...'

I began to think that this was growing into a Russian tragedy and that we should all have to weep or drink a bottle of vodka soon, so I put an end to it by holding out my hand and saying good night.

The Russian officer shook my hand and then both he and the orderly saluted smartly. I did my best to reciprocate, but was at a considerable disadvantage in a crumpled pair of not very clean pyjamas which had been doing constant duty for a fortnight, and struggling against continual travelling, dust and dirt. My bare feet did not make me feel any smarter, and my hair was tousled.

Saluting as they went, they withdrew. As they went out through the door, just for the fun of it, I called after them 'Good night' in Russian. They turned and looked at me. Eyes talk. Theirs said, 'So the blighter knows Russian after all.'

I returned to bed, and the waiter came back a few minutes later. He said that the Russian officer had said that if he did not come back I would know that the Commandant was satisfied and that everything was all right. I said, 'If they do come back, for heaven's sake give them a bottle of vodka at my expense and make them tight and see them home and tell them to come back at eight o'clock in the morning, by which time I hope I shall have put a trail of dust fifty miles long between myself and this township.'

He continued to tell me that the Russians had not come to the pub to see me. They had come to disarm two Persian officers who were in mufti and were carrying revolvers. Then, seeing my car, had made inquiries about it, and had not believed the waiter when he had told them that it belonged to a British officer who was staying the night in the place.

This is a long and tedious story, but Russian stories can be long and tedious.

While I was in Meshed, Clarmont Skrine, the British Indian Consul-General, insisted that, as someone interested in things Persian, I should take an afternoon off and pay a visit with him to the great Mohammedan shrine of Imam Reza in Meshed. I wrote:

I had the good fortune to visit the shrine here with Mr Skrine. It is the most important shrine in Persia, the tomb of the Imam Reza, and one of the most important Mohammedan places of pilgrimage. As I topped a rise and saw the golden dome and minarets glinting in the late evening sunlight, I could not help thinking of the countless thousands of pilgrims whose hearts had been elevated by that sight over many centuries as they ended a long journey of hundreds, and perhaps thousands, of miles – which must often have represented a life's savings – to visit the sacred place. Before the time of the ex-Shah, who forbade many of the old religious customs, many of the faithful also brought their relatives to Meshed to bury them near the shrine. They say that if you dig down a few feet anywhere in Meshed you will find human bones.

Until a few years ago it was impossible for an unbeliever to enter the shrine, but the ex-Shah secularised the foundation, broke the power of the old hierarchy of priests who controlled it, and placed it under Government supervision. It is enormously wealthy.

The tile work, the exquisite chromatic architecture, and the golden dome and minarets and, above all, the lovely porticos reflecting in their gold roofs the bright glowing sunlight off the ground below are very impressive indeed.

After seeing the buildings themselves, which are very extensive, we visited the treasure rooms. We were shown some of their antique carpets and embroidery, all of it several hundred years old. It is really some of the loveliest work I have ever seen. The taste, the designs and the colours are perfect.

We then visited the library, which has over 18,000 books. We were shown some of the treasures. First an illustrated pharmacopoeia over 700 years old on cotton paper. The ink of the manuscript was in perfect condition, and the drawings of plants and animals were most interesting, and the colours must be as good as the day they were painted. Then some illuminated volumes of the Koran, and other books. They are real treasures and works of art. There was one volume of the Koran which had 600 pages, the margin of each decorated with a different design, each a complete

work of the miniature painter's art. They say that it is estimated that it must have taken at least two months to do
each page.

From the point of view of my Intelligence work my visit was
successful, and I was able to agree plans with my carpet seller
subordinate for that area who met me there. We also arranged
to meet again in a few days on the road south towards Zahidan
to do some more planning there

Central Persia is a vast desert, the northern part known as
the Dasht-i-Kavir and the southern part as the Dasht-i-Lut. It
was because it was of particular interest to me that I decided to
cross it on my way back from Meshed, from east to west right
in the middle between the two halves. I wanted to judge
whether a German army could cross it. It was convenient for
me to make the journey on my way back to Kerman from
Meshed. On 13 September 1942 I wrote from Yezd on the
south west side of the desert:

I finally left Meshed on 8 September and, after a false start,
and after making heavy weather of an easy journey of 180
miles, reached a little place called Gunabad, on the Meshed-
Zahidan road, that night. I had some supper and went to bed
and was then systematically phlebotomised till dawn by an
insatiable swarm of sandflies.

Next morning I left Gunabad to cross the great desert. It
was a very interesting journey. It is still fairly hot, and there
is a good lot of rough going which is fatiguing. The route
takes off from the main Meshed road a couple of hundred
miles south of Meshed and then cuts through a place named
Tabas and fetches up at Yezd which is on the west edge of the
desert and is on the main Kerman-Isfahan road. Almost the
whole area it passes through is a completely dry, barren
wilderness, the route itself skirts along ranges of mountains
and very seldom comes down to the floor of the desert.
Indeed there is only one stretch of a dozen miles or so where
you feel that you are really crossing the floor of the main

desert. The route is always in sight of high mountains, and you are never 'out of sight of land'.

Leaving in the early morning, we had a really lovely drive for a hundred miles or so. The atmosphere was crystal clear. There was a blue sky, and the colouring of the hills was beautiful. But, as we drew westwards, the pastel colours and clear sky of the Persian plateau gradually faded. The sky became brassy, and all colours were smudged into the dull, oppressive, grey heat of the desert. The country became more barren. Then, after passing through a gorge in a high range of mountains, we came out in the late afternoon onto the plain of Tabas.

Here, in the midst of the great Persian desert, is a wide, low-lying, hot, sandy plain, strewn with groves of date palms. The town of Tabas itself is in the middle of the plain. Its most noteworthy feature to the hot and weary traveller is a small formal garden on the Moghul pattern in which full use is made of a small stream of water with a good head. The garden is cool and shady and has fountains playing in it, and two little waterfalls. A miniature Shalimar. A most unexpected diminutive paradise in the midst of this howling wilderness.

I spent the night in a caravanserai in the little town. But, after arriving and cleaning myself as best I could, I walked about the town to have a good look at this extraordinary oasis. The Persians are very hospitable people, and one of the inhabitants spoke to me and, when I told him I was putting up at the caravanserai, invited me to supper with him and his family, an invitation I very readily accepted. I had a very pleasant evening with them. The father told me that Tabas had exported something which had become well known in Britain – the Tabas cat, corrupted to Tabby cat. The man's wife, like so many Persian women, was very bright, and great fun, and she spoke very fast. Your Persian needs to be good to keep up with the Persian girls. Her husband had visited

India a few times. He was very pro-British. He was well informed about the war – from the wireless – and was equally anti-German.

I returned to the caravanserai for the night. The next day was a long, wearisome and hot, through very desolate country. At length, two hours after nightfall, we reached another caravanserai where we put up for the night. Here there was quite a good stream of brackish waster, and a cistern of fresh water for drinking.

If an artist wanted to paint a picture of *The Gates of Hell*, he could not do better than to take for his model a bit of that country. A day's march on a hot, dusty track stretching away before him across a barren plain of steep and endless undulations to a gap in a ridge of bare and broken jagged rock peaks. And beyond, ranges of mad, Dantesque, crumbling spires of naked rock, the colour of cinders. In the foreground, a grill of red-black stones on yellow-red clay. And over all a burning sun in a sky of molten bronze. Here lies the bare and broken spine of Persia. Its flesh, long since torn from it by hot winds, and washed down by countless ages of occasional very heavy rain storms, lies rotting in the lowest parts of the desert in the form of a soft pink-white, salty, treacherous mud, known as the Kavir.

I was unusually tired when we reached the caravanserai, so I had a little food and went to bed. We had been too busy to attempt to eat since an early breakfast. Caravanserais are not restful places. In the summer everyone sleeps on the roofs of the courtyard to keep cool, and they talk and smoke opium and drink tea till far into the night. If there are women about they chatter in high-pitched voices, and babies cry. At about 4 a.m. two cocks in the courtyard started crowing, followed by a donkey braying. Then, with first light, a muezzin on the roof of the far side of the courtyard starting calling the faithful to prayer. That was the end of all sleep for the unbeliever, but the faithful, well soaked in opium, with its head wrapped tightly in a blanket and its feet sticking out at the other end, slept on profoundly.

Morier, in his book *The Adventures of Hajji Baba of Ispahan*, describes how Hajji Baba, when he was the servant of the court doctor Mirza Ahmak, was sent on a mission to the European doctor who was visiting the court with a foreign mission. Hajji Baba did not know quite how he ought to tackle the Farangi doctor so asked his own master for some advice. He was told that the one thing he must remember was that all Farangis were most peculiarly inverted. They were in every way the exact opposite of Persians. He then gave Hajji Baba this catalogue of differences:

'Their manners and customs are totally different to ours, that is true,' replied Mirza Ahmak, 'and you may form some idea of them, when I tell you, that instead of shaving their heads, and letting their beards grow, as we do, they do the very contrary, for not a vestige of hair is to be seen on their chins, and their hair is as thick on their heads as if they had made a vow never to cut it off: then they sit on little platforms, whilst we squat on the ground; they take up their food with claws made of iron, whilst we use our fingers; they are always walking about, we keep seated; they wear tight clothes, we loose ones; they write from left to right, we from right to left; they never pray, we five times a day; in short, there is no end to what might be related of them; but most certain it is, that they are the most filthy people on the earth, for they hold nothing to be unclean; they eat all sorts of animals, from a pig to a tortoise, without the least scruple, and that without first cutting their throats; they will dissect a dead body, without requiring any purification after it, and perform all the brute functions of their nature, without ever thinking it necessary to go to the hot bath, or even rubbing themselves with sand after them.'

'And is it true,' said I, 'that they are so irascible, that if perchance their word is doubted, and they are called liars, they will fight on such an occasion till they die?'

'That is also said of them,' answered the doctor; 'but the case has not happened to me yet; however, I must warn you of one thing, which is, that if they happen to admire anything that you possess, you must not say to them, as you would to one of us, "It is a present to you, it is your property", lest they should take you at your word and keep it, which you know would be inconvenient, and not what you intended; but you must endeavour as much as possible to speak what you think, for that is what they like.'

However, one thing the author, Morier, did not mention was the difference in the use of the blanket. We always sleep with our heads out and our feet in, and the Persians with their heads wrapped up and their feet out in the cold. Perhaps, if we had inherited from our ancestors feet hardened by centuries of sharp rocks and burning sand, and lived in a country where muezzins perform violent vocal exercises at crack of dawn, we should do the same.

Towards sunset that evening we had come upon a man walking in the direction we were going. We stopped and gave him a lift. He was a weedy-looking youth suffering from trachoma. He said he was carrying the post from Tabas to Yezd. Usually it was carried by a man on a camel but he was sick, so this youth was doing the job on foot. He had no water with him, but carried a water melon to quench his thirst. He said that he had not come the route we had come but had taken a short cut across the hills. Even so, as the crow flies, I made out from the map (such as it is) that he had come not less than thirty miles that day, and it was probably more like thirty-five. He did not appear to be tired or thirsty.

When we arrived at the caravanserai he had a small glass of tea; discovered that there was a donkey there which belonged to a man who lived a few stages further on, and wanted it brought on to him; put his heavy pack on his back, and started off again without any rest. Next morning we passed him at 8.30 a.m., thirty-two miles further on, walking and driving the reluctant donkey before him.

About midday we came upon a little constructed pond in the middle of the desert. It had a little water in it. There was a grey wagtail there. What on earth was it doing in the midst of the desert?

Having left the caravanserai early, we reached Yezd in the afternoon, hungry, thirsty and fairly tired. Perhaps I may have been the first Briton to traverse the great Persian desert, the Dasht-i-Kavir.

Yesterday I had my hair cut. The barber told me his life's history with commendable brevity. He is at present in the hard luck state. A Persian is usually either on top of the world or deep in the trough. Like so many of them he had travelled a lot and spoke three languages fluently. I think that the habit of Persians travelling about their own huge country has worn off the edge of novelty in travel for them. Many of them go abroad without considering it unusual or adventurous. Nor is it considered unusual to have a knowledge of foreign languages, because several languages are spoken within Persia itself. The traveller could quite well get along here without any knowledge of Persian provided he knew other languages. Most useful would be Turkish and Russian. There are many people who speak one or other or both. And in most places someone can be found who knows either English or French. The barber examined my head like a carver wondering where to make the first cut in the joint. Then, poking my crown with his comb, asked me if I had shaved my tonsure. Rather unkind, I thought, to one trying manfully to hide the bald patches!

From Kerman, 16 September 1942, to Maxine:

I arrived back here yesterday evening, and hope to stay here for a little. I am very well indeed but feel I would like to have a rest from travelling. Otherwise I shall get stale, and I have a lot more to do in the coming months.

I did not mention anything to you about the murder of Mr Harris, the vice-consul in Isfahan, and Dr Griffith, the missionary doctor, as I thought you might not have noticed it in the Indian papers, and that it might worry you to know that such things are possible. Actually there was nothing to it. Harris disobeyed the rules, and the whole party paid for it. He took an unescorted party into a known dangerous tribal area, carrying arms, the day after the local tribesmen had had a battle with Persian troops. The fact that he was carrying arms which are always useful to lawless tribesmen was quite enough to get him murdered. It would be about as sensible for one of us to walk off into Waziristan alone carrying a ·303 rifle.

I did not know Harris, but I knew Griffith, a very nice man, and a great loss to the mission. You need not worry about that. Most of the tribes in Persia are harmless. They may rob you, but the murder of Europeans is extremely rare. Round here everything is perfectly quiet. We have not even had one of our mild robberies on the roads for a long time. The bad tribes are in west Persia. It was in that country that Harris and Griffith were killed.

I am taking every opportunity to get as fit as I can. I walk everywhere rather than drive or cycle, and I have a good walk nearly every evening. A little over a mile from my house is a good line of rocky hills rising about a thousand feet above this. It has endless good scrambles on it so, in the evening, I put on a pair of gym shoes, run most of the way there and back and spend half an hour or more scrambling. I shall gradually increase my exertions, and shall do some long distance work carrying a heavy pack, as I am hoping, and expecting, to get the chance to return to being an honest-to-God soldier.

From Kerman, 17 September 1942:

I had meant to go to bed early last night but just as I was thinking of turning in there came a loud knocking at the door of the courtyard. The servants had all gone to bed, so I went to open the door myself. It was the Consulate Indian Head Clerk in his pyjamas. He lives quite close to me. He said that he had just had a telephone message from the city to say that a big fire was raging, and to ask whether we could offer any assistance. We live about a mile out of the town. I ran up to the Sappers' mess, and found them just about to go to bed. They had no fire-fighting equipment, but they collected some of their men and we set off for the fire. It was a lovely, fresh, moonlit night with thin wisps of white clouds in the sky. As bright as only it can be in a desert country. We could soon see the fire. Seventy tons of bales of cotton were blazing in the store of a spinning mill which there is here. There is, of course, practically no water in the town and had the fire spread it might have been very serious, as there has been no rain since last winter and everything is as dry as matchwood.

However, the building, though almost in the middle of the town, was isolated from the neighbouring buildings. It had thick walls of sun-baked mud bricks, and the roof was a brick dome covered with dried mud. There was, therefore, not much to burn except the cotton inside. There was no wind and no sparks so, as the roof did not collapse, there was very little chance of the fire spreading, though sheets of flame were pouring through the windows. The whole building was just one great brick oven with a roaring furnace inside. Even had there been water available nothing could have been done to save the store by the time we got there. The Persians had the matter well in hand. A large crowd was watching, but there was no excitement or noise. I am always struck by how calm and well-mannered the Persians are, whatever the circumstances may be. The Chief of Police was conducting operations. There was nothing to do but let the fire burn itself out, and to take timely action should it look like spreading. He had made arrangements to divert a small stream, which runs through our gardens, into the city, but actually the water did not reach the scene of the fire till 3 a.m. When it was obvious that there was nothing we could do, he thanked us for turning out, and said that we might as well go back to bed. I told him to send a message if he wanted us again, and we went home.

I have been away for a couple of days. I was down on the edge of the desert where I spent the night with an Assyrian road contractor, who has an establishment there, with whom I have often stayed before.

I did not recruit him to work for me. He was just a friend. He was a Christian and it was his ambition to make enough money to build a cathedral. He was a very competent, resourceful and efficient man.

His men have a tame wild pig. It was sweet when it was small, and is still very attractive. It spends most of its time in the cookhouse, and sleeps with the cook who has taught it some tricks. I suppose the poor creature will have to be slaughtered when he grows his tusks, as he will be dangerous even if he does not mean to be. They also have a tame fox, and a tame violinist. He is a new acquisition. He was till recently the leader of an orchestra, but has taken to driving a lorry as he finds it more paying. The world is out of joint indeed. He has his violin with him, as he says that if he does a week without practising his fingers get stiff. He played to us after supper.

I slept in a room with a couple of Sappers. They have some first class chaps here. One of them had a gramophone and was trying to learn a sloppy French song from a record he had bought in Teheran. We did not go to bed till after midnight, and I went to sleep with the gramophone still wailing the French song. I was woken up next morning at 6.30 by the gramophone, which had started again complaining, 'J'attendrai le jour et la nuit ... j'attendrai ton retour, etc.' I got up and said I was off into the desert to look for some peace!

When I returned to Kerman Clinton-Thomas had been posted elsewhere – regretfully for me, because I liked him very much. I took over the rent of his house. Two new vice-consuls arrived, Major Mohamed Hassan, a Muslim whom I invited to share my house, and Nicholson, who lived in the consulate. They were able and agreeable people. Hassan was destined to hold senior ambassadorial appointments in the Pakistan diplomatic service; and to him I am indebted for the gift of the four volumes of Edward Browne's *Literary History of Persia*, a work comparable to Edward Gibbon's *Decline and Fall of the Roman Empire*.

I was able to get BBC news on a wireless set, and was naturally following the war news with interest and concern. It affected my own outlook on what I was doing. I had, of course, to take my orders from the Government of India, but I was also in a position to influence their opinions and decision-making. The question I was following most closely was: 'Are the Germans going to succeed in overcoming Russian resistance in south Russia and in breaking through the Caucasus?' In my letter of 12 October 1942 to Maxine, I outlined my tentative thinking:

> The war news is good. We are at the beginning of winter and the Germans have abandoned their attack on Stalingrad. Their casualties must have been enormous, and their exhausted armies will suffer terribly this winter. They are virtually beaten unless any disaster overtakes Russia during the winter. Russia has lost her most productive grain areas. She has also lost half her population. They must, one would think, be facing a serious food problem. However there is a difference between Russia and Germany in this respect. The Germans, as a nation, have been used for generations to being well fed, and they will suffer severely from a shortage of food or bad food. The Russians have been used always to

famines, food shortage and hard fare, and there is no doubt that their soldiers can thrive on rations which would be a real hardship to the Germans.

I am glad to have your good news of Thomas, but am sorry I am not seeing him grow up. I feel that he changes more quickly at his present age than at any other.

In the autumn of 1942 the Kerman Consulate received from the Legation in Teheran a sum of money for local relief work. With my penchant for voluntary jobs such as mess secretary, I told Arthur Barlow, the Consul, that I would organise this if he liked. He agreed. I was satisfied that it would not interfere with my work because all it needed was an organisational plan, and a good Persian, whom I had in mind, to do the detailed day-to-day running. Moreover, anything that widened my contacts, and fostered goodwill towards me in the local community, was of potential value to my work. On 7 November 1942 I wrote to Maxine:

I had a very lovely day yesterday. I have taken on a spare time job here of feeding daily a thousand of the poor of Kerman, for which the British Government has provided funds. I'm not much good at business, but am doing what I can to get supplies as cheaply as possible out of this starving countryside. We are setting up a kitchen and are providing one good cooked meal per day. I have bought meat on the hoof sufficient to do for three months. I was yesterday trying to get fuel cheaply, and my search took me to a really lovely little village in the mountains some thirty miles from here. There are the most surprising little places in these barren mountains. This was just like a little bit of Kashmir. It was a really beautiful bright crisp autumn day, with a warm sun and long, hard, black shadows. We sat on a bench with a sparkling stream running between its legs, under a golden walnut tree and had our lunch of curds, dates, fried eggs and bread, with the head man of the village. A picnic like that is usually pleasant in Persia, because the Persians themselves so enjoy it. They love nature. They glory in the fine days and lovely views and beautiful colours, and their conversation and jokes are very like our own. For instance, we had a small boy with us, and when he had stuffed himself in silence for about half an hour and I said that I must really arrange for him to see a doctor on account of his failing appetite, everyone laughed and pulled his leg just as we might do.

I have had a succession of callers, one of them a hard cuss whom I sent out today to clinch the bargain for firewood. By enlisting our own labour and cutting from the mountainside what God grows in the way of dry roots of bushes, and by obtaining some valuable help from well-wishers, it looks as though I shall get it to the cooking-pot at about a seventh of the price firewood now costs in the town here. It will probably burn about twice as fast as tree wood, so, in the end, we may have our firing for about a third of the estimated cost. I shall believe it when I see the pot on the boil.

I'm always damn soft over my own money, but I'm going to be as hard as nails over this money and fill as many wretched hungry bellies as I can and not waste a penny.

My own winter supply of firewood has now arrived, or rather half of it has. It is nearly all wood of fruit trees. Walnut, apricot, fig and some chenar. It is all brought in from the hills on donkeys and, to save weight, a pack saddle is not used. Instead the wood is packed on pads of soft bushes and grasses. Mine was packed for the most part on what appears to be a kind of wild lavender. This is thrown in with the wood, or at least they weigh as much of it in with the wood as you let them. So you can imagine what my wood store smells like full of fruit wood and wild lavender. It is a real pleasure to be in it. I am now setting about getting an axe. I shall then be able to enjoy the agreeable task of chopping it up.

From Kerman, 12 November 1942, to Maxine:

This morning I received your most distressing letter about Sprag's death, which was a great shock.

I have written to your Pa. I am most terribly sorry for you both. It will be a terrible blow to him after all he has been through, and particularly after the strain of the past few months. What awful bad luck after getting through the battles, and surviving his capture and journey to Italy, and with the war as it is now with brighter prospects for an early release of our prisoners in Italy.

Sprag Mitchell had, as we learnt very much later from a fellow prisoner of war, been shot when trying to escape. His death was a great loss not only to the future of the family but also to many other people. He was an exceedingly nice and attractive person of unusual charm, much liked by everyone and with a host of friends. He had a light-hearted ebullience which enlivened any company. He was also held in high regard and affection by his brother officers, and his men in the Gunners.

The loss to Maxine was grievous in the extreme. He was her only brother and she had no sister. He alone shared her childhood memories. Likewise a grievous blow to her widower father – his only son. War casualties are usually a matter of statistics, but each and every one is a heartache to someone.

The news still seems excellent. I have just heard on the wireless that indications from Moscow are that their ring round Stalingrad has been closed. Too early yet, of course, to know how the battle will go, and the Germans cannot have failed to foresee the possibility of such an offensive and must have some plan. However, it all seems to have prospects of the absolute ham-stringing of the German land forces. If the Russians smash up 25 of their divisions in that area, presumably their best troops, they will have taken the sting out of Hitler's army.

From Kerman, 6 December 1942:

Our feeding of the poor is going well. We now feed 800 daily, and I hope to be able to put it up to 1,000 as we have almost secured enough food now to last us three months, and have some cash in hand. In this crowd of beggars one sees the fundamental character of the Persians. I doubt that anywhere else in the world you could find such orderliness, dignity and good manners in a crowd of people in such an appalling state of destitution.

The south coast of Persia was in my area. I could not neglect it. It was a region crucial in Alexander the Great's debacle. I described a visit to it:

I had a trip to Bandar Abbas, the minute port on the Persian coast at the entrance to the Persian Gulf. It is rather hot and malarious but has interesting historical associations.

Opposite it in the Gulf is the island of Hormuz, which was once one of the wealthiest ports in the East. It was mentioned many times by Milton on account of its fabulous wealth. It was captured by the Portuguese, whom we later drove out of it. In one of our attacks on it the famous English sailor and discoverer Baffin who gave his name to Baffin Bay, was killed. He appears to have been a gunner for, according to the historian of the time, he went ashore 'with his geometrical instruments' to take readings for 'the better levelling his peece' to take a shot at the fort, when one of the defenders hit him in the belly with a small shot and 'he gave three leaps, by account, and died at once'. That was the end of poor Master Baffin.

The old Portuguese fort is still on the island, which is now almost uninhabited, there being only one small village on it. The fort is in ruins, and only the underground water cisterns are fairly well preserved. They were necessary as the island has no water except what it can collect from a very small rainfall. Over the years the inhabitants have removed most of the timber from the walls, as there is no timber or natural fuel on the island – with the result that much of the walling has collapsed. Some of the old guns are still there. It is interesting how much coral is used in the building of the walls.

We did later manage to place a stay-behind agent in the vicinity of Bandar Abbas.

I borrowed a boat and six stout sailors and went out at dawn one morning for a few hours' fishing. We sailed out a few miles as there was a breeze. Needless to say the breeze dropped later and we rowed some very hot miles home again.

The sailors said there are always fish to be caught, but that the best fishing is some miles further than I had time to go. The tackle was awful; just hand lines and a few rusty hooks. However we baited our hooks with a kind of large sardine which lives in those waters, and proceeded to fish. We caught some very nice fish with pink scales which turned out to be very good eating.

If the Duke of Wellington could take a pack of hounds to the Peninsular Wars for his recreation, I reckoned that I could treat myself to an hour or two fishing before the real work of the day started. Moreover, the acquaintance of some seafaring men and fisherfolk could be of use to me.

I had fixed with the authorities in Delhi towards the end of December 1942 to return to India for consultation with them. I particularly wanted to talk to George Jenkin, the Director of Intelligence in the Bureau who had initiated the idea of sending me to Persia. (His name was William and he was later knighted as Sir William Jenkin, but he was always known as George.)

By the end of 1942 I had completed my mission and set up a trained 'stay-behind' organisation to deal with the situation if the German forces should break through the Caucasus and attack India through east and central Persia. But I was one of those who felt that we should not waste – or expend – more than the minimum of effort and resources on defensive measures once the tide was turned against the Germans, and I believed that the events in south east Russia at the end of November 1942 marked the turning point. The German 6th Army appeared to be caught in the Russian trap at Stalingrad, and the Russian strategy forced Hitler to withdraw the forces with which he would have broken through the Caucasus, for fear that they also should be wiped out. It seemed to me therefore that, far from continuing to reinforce my Persian arrangements, I ought to be thinking of winding them up. It was this I wanted to discuss in Delhi.

I got qualified agreement for my proposal, but nothing was to be done to wind up my organisation unless and until the Germans at Stalingrad finally surrendered – which they did a month or so later, at the beginning of February 1942.

But for myself personally, things were not going the way I wanted. There was something of a tug-of-war over me between the Army and the Indian Intelligence Bureau. George Jenkin said that it was imperative that I should move to Teheran if the east Persian organisation was wound up, and there intensify my efforts on extending the Silver case (which, as I explained in chapter 1, was a double agent operation whereby the Intelligence Bureau in Delhi were feeding false information to the German legation in Kabul, Afghanistan) and help the local security people in Persia to mop up the German stay-behind organisation.

My letter of 25 January 1943 to Maxine made it clear that I was not without anxieties about her and Thomas. She had decided to send him to the hills for the hot weather with his nurse. She felt that she herself ought to remain in Delhi and continue her work in Army Headquarters.

From Kerman, 5 February 1943:

I am so sorry I did not get a letter to you last week but I was flat on my back, *hors de combat* with some sort of fever, for seven days. I'm not right yet, but now have a normal temperature most of the time, and can get out of bed and crawl around a bit. It will take me another week or ten days, but I am well on the mend. I don't think there was anything the matter with me, just a persistent temperature and a persistent bad head and complete loss of appetite. I thought it might be jaundice, but the doctor says you can't have it twice and anyhow it wasn't. I think it was just one of the unaccountable fevers when the body gets sick of itself and decides to turn over a new leaf and does it rather violently and probably leaves one all the better.

There are two mission doctors here. A man, who is down with diphtheria, and a woman. She visited me and was really very decent.

I haven't managed much in the way of invalid food. Having eaten nothing at all for four days, I began to dream of sausage rolls and things so thought it was time to try some food. I told the bearer and my cook to prepare me something light for lunch. 'Certainly. Nothing easier.' At length it was announced as ready, so I told them to bring it. The first course consisted of a chunk of fried mutton (probably goat) with a fried beetroot alongside. I spread it round the plate for a bit with a fork to show I had taken some interest in it, and then asked if there was anything else. 'Rather! Pudding.' 'Well, bring it along.' It came. A chunk of fried cake. The cook said it had been lying idle for a week or so and it seemed a pity to waste it.

From Zahidan, 6 March 1943:

About myself, as far as I can gather I am off to Teheran soon for a short time. I will let you know address etc. later. This does not suit me as I am determined to get to Burma where I feel I could be useful.

The weather has been very unsettled. Yesterday I motored here (Zahidan) from Kerman, about 330 miles. [I went to meet a member of the Quetta Intelligence Bureau to discuss the winding up of my stay-behind organisation when Delhi came up with agreement to do so.] We descended the long slope to the desert. I have seldom seen the desert looking more menacing. There was a steady wind from the west and the sand was creeping in its horrible way along the desert floor, like a swarm of hopper locusts, filling ruts and holes

[57]

and creeping on; climbing stones and mounds, piling itself up on the leeward side and creeping on again. Sand does not pile up on the side it strikes an obstacle, but on the far side. It was hot and hazy and the air was full of dust. We took off most of our clothes. With two-thirds of the road behind us, we stopped in the middle of the desert and ate a sandy lunch. It then looked as though a dust storm was coming up behind us so we beat it and arrived here about an hour after sunset.

I had a lovely drive to Teheran today. About a hundred miles south of Teheran is the town of Qum, the only town of any size in the 270 miles between Isfahan and Teheran. It is a famous place of pilgrimage. The shrine is very rich and is one of the few with a gold dome. It is the tomb of Fatimah, sister of the Imam Reza, whose famous tomb is at Meshed. Hajji Baba sought refuge in Fatimah's shrine from probable execution after it had been discovered that he had made a slave girl in the Shah's harem pregnant.

Coming from the south the road climbs over a ridge and looking down from the top you see the little town below you with the golden dome sparkling in the sunlight. And, if you're lucky – I was today – away behind, a hundred miles to the north, you see the high snow-capped Elburz mountains. They were lovely: standing up from the red plain they just floated in the sky as the blue lower slopes merged in tone and colour with the sky itself. There was the faintest haze which gave the long line of snows a pink tint. And, towering 6,000 feet above the other peaks, stood the conical volcanic Demavand, doing its best to out-Fuji Fujiyama. It really is a very beautiful mountain.

I have not yet heard anything definite about myself, but feel I should get some orders fairly soon. I am therefore in a restless state.

From Kerman, 22 March 1943:

I am, as you see, back in Kerman. I don't know yet what is likely to happen to me. I think that any regular officer of the

Indian Army who can possibly be spared who is not in or about Burma with the troops these days is wasting his time and his knowledge and experience, and that is where I intend to get to if I possibly can. We have been on the defensive, which means a lot more thinking behind than fighting in front. Now we are on the offensive, and the more ground that can be made in front, the smaller will become the problems behind, and every man of us who has had all the military service I have had should be in the front. I only hope that I can persuade other people, particularly George Jenkin, that I am right. Knowing that I am, perhaps I can.

I have had orders today to pack up and go and squat in Teheran. My own feelings I shall suppress. I have exerted what pressure I can to get something more active. Possibly even I have exceeded the limits of discretion. Now I must get on with what I have got to do and hope that the future will not let me down.

The fact was that the Indian authorities were still very sensitive about Persia. Unexpected things can happen in war. There might yet be a German recovery in Russia with a renewed threat to the Caucasus. Wars are not won until one side or the other has capitulated. Victory can be snatched from the jaws of defeat. Britain survived Dunkirk to be victorious. The Russians had suffered appalling losses. Might not the Germans still overwhelm them?

It was therefore considered too early to wind down my operations in east and south Persia. However it was accepted that they could be put on hold, and I was ordered to Teheran for two purposes. One to be in a position to help with the Silver case. The other to help the PAIFORCE people mop up the underground Germans; this was very important because they posed a serious threat particularly to the vital rail communications to Russia from the Persian Gulf, and also because they might be able to report our military dispositions, and lack of them, to Berlin. It was in fact right to leave me in Persia, and I was to acknowledge the fact a little later on. What I had to do had indeed to be done, and there was no one else with all the necessary qualifications and experience to relieve me. Nevertheless, understandably I think, I wanted to return to the command of troops in the active war theatre of most concern to India; that is to say the Burma campaign.

Meanwhile I messed and worked with the small PAIFORCE security unit in Teheran which was trying to mop up the German underground organisation.

From Teheran, 6 April 1943:

Not being a city dweller, I was woken up this morning by the first motor which passed the window. I suppose I shall soon learn to sleep through the noise, but I am no lover of cities.

I am attached to PAIFORCE, and wives (unless they were already domiciled here before the war) are not allowed. The Army very wisely does not argue over these things or make any exceptions. I am sorry George Jenkin was so stupid as to raise your hopes.

George Jenkin was a wily person and developed and nurtured his contacts in other departments carefully. I was one of the Army people whom he had come to know well and wanted to keep in his orbit. I suppose he thought that if he could get Maxine to Teheran to be with me, that would keep me quiet for the time being. From the wider point of view, and not from the point of view of my own narrower personal interests, he was in fact right to keep me where I was in Persia, and he thereafter had plans for my further use which he did not divulge to me or to anyone else at the time. He was fighting his war in his own way. I liked him very much, and greatly enjoyed working with such an able and professional man, but I was not blind to the fact that he was a crafty old thing.

I heard a very nice saying from a Persian the morning I left Kerman. He came round to say goodbye to me. He said, 'I suppose you will be in Yezd tonight.' I replied that it was much more likely that I should be stuck in the mud on the road somewhere for the next ten days, as it had just started to drizzle. 'It won't be much,' he said. 'It is only weeping for your departure. It never rains hard once spring has come.' Then he mentioned a charming saying which I had not heard before. 'In Persia', he said, 'we have a saying that the spring has only two moods, either weeping or laughing.'

From Teheran, 10 May 1943:

The news is splendid. With North Africa finished, we shall have enormous forces released for our coming offensive on Europe.

As we are now working summer hours, which means clocking in at 6 a.m., I sometimes have a snooze in the afternoon. I was lying in bed the other afternoon, with a sheet over me, ruminating, and about to get up, when someone came into the house and walked into the sitting room which has a glass door (frosted) leading to my room. I thought it was Tett, my landlord. Suddenly the door opened and a woman walked in. Maintaining my composure, I said, 'Good afternoon.' 'Good afternoon,' she replied. 'I presume', I said, 'that you are looking for Mr Tett.' 'No,' she said, 'I am looking for some furniture.' 'Well,' I said, 'if you give me ten minutes to get up, you can do all the looking you like.' 'Oh no,' she replied, looking round. 'There's nothing here I want.' She drank a glass of water. I said 'Good afternoon', and she went out.

Next afternoon I passed her in the street. I was in mufti and, being well brought up, I took off my hat as I passed and said, 'Good afternoon.' She looked puzzled, trying to recall where she had seen that face and heard that 'Good afternoon' before.

I have since established her identity, and I gather that gentlemen's bedrooms are no novelty to her.

Now I bolt the door.

4
Teheran at War

On 6 June 1943 I wrote to Maxine from Teheran:

I expect George will have told you that I arrived here safely on the first. It was a marvellous journey and I thoroughly enjoyed every minute of it. It certainly is the way to travel. The flying boat part of it is the best fun and the most comfortable, and the BOAC certainly look after one very well. The colours in the Gulf are particularly fascinating. If I have to come to India again, I shall certainly try to come by air instead of this awful motoring.

On Saturday night an eccentric American friend in Teheran took me on a round of the cafés, which I had not done before. One of the cafés we visited had really quite a good and cheerful cabaret. All the girls were European except one. I was really rather horrified when a Persian girl came on inadequately clad, and did a most lecherous dance. She was reminiscent of the 2,000-year-old carvings at Persepolis – 'The courts where Jamshid gloried and drank deep'. It was saddening to see the daughter of a 5,000-year-old civilisation, endowed with all the grace of form and figure of centuries of fine breeding, so debase herself for the pleasure of a foreign audience, for not one per cent of the clientele was Persian.

We visited altogether four cafés. The standard was quite good, and they were quiet, clean and decent. Fortunately everything closes early. There was an early curfew here, but it has now been extended to 11 p.m.

It is really quite hot here now. The temperature is over a hundred, but it cools down in the evening and is very pleasant sitting out in the garden. I sleep on the roof and usually need a blanket by about 4 a.m. Altogether I feel very lucky not to be in some ruddy place like Baghdad.

Life is more interesting than it promised to be, and I am fairly reconciled to it as a temporary measure.

That reflects the progress we were making in dealing with the German underground organisation.

I am very sorry to hear that your cousin Tony is missing [Tony Harper, Maxine's first cousin]. I am afraid it will be a terrible blow for his mother. There is not much wrong when a person like him, physically handicapped and obviously nervous, went out on operational flying. [He was lost in a bombing raid over Germany, and was never heard of again.]

My future of course is, as always, obscure, but I should say the chances are that I shall be here for some time. George wants me here for the present and I think these people here would press for me to remain at any rate for the next few months, simply on the principle of 'the devil you know ...', and because I do my best to be helpful and cooperative. I personally feel that I shall be here till about Christmas at least.

I went to Lar, a valley on the northern side of the Elburz mountains where the Legation has a camp, and where the British colony have camped every summer for the last fifty years or so. It is a really lovely valley some 8,000–9,000 feet up; very like the High Himalayas. Through it runs the Lar river, a beautiful green-blue river with a gravel bed and full of trout. I only got one afternoon's fishing as it takes the best part of a day to get into the valley. It was then another eight miles' walk to the fishing. However, I caught twenty-seven trout in the afternoon, and would have caught fifty if I had known the river well, and had been fishing better, but I am out of practice. Four of us caught 100 trout in the afternoon. They were all small. Very good eating. It was lovely walking up to one's knees in sweet-smelling grass along the river bank.

The valley was full of horses as the Persian Army summers its breeding establishment up there. They are really only little things about 14 hands, even less, but they looked very pretty grazing loose in the meadows. Standing right up over the valley is the beautiful mountain Demavand with his head in a cloud most of the day, and clear and sharp, snow-covered and cold, in the light of the full moon at night.

I must have walked the best part of thirty-five miles in three days; not much, but I haven't done any lengthy walking since we were in Kulu so I felt pleasantly stiff and tired, and got much sunburnt. I arrived back feeling weary of limb, but refreshed in soul, and it seemed as though I had been away a month from this infernal stuffy city. I brought back a couple of dozen trout which we ate with relish for breakfast this morning.

The war is going well. It looks as though Sicily and 400,000 Axis troops will be in the bag before long, and Italy virtually out of the war. With the Russians threatening the centre of the German front in Russia, and with presumably much heavier pressure to come from us once Sicily is cleared up, it looks at last like the beginning of the end.

Churchill put it correctly. It was not the beginning of the end. It was the end of the beginning.

Colonel Geoffrey Wheeler, an old acquaintance of mine, came on a visit from Delhi where he had his headquarters. Among other duties, he was responsible for publicity material directed at Persia, and he produced a well got up glossy magazine in Persian called *Shaipoor – The Trumpet*.

I asked him whether he had any underlying publicity theme – what I think is technically known as 'the editorial line'.

'Yes,' he replied, 'busts and battleships.'

We were having mounting successes against the German underground organisation. But their leader, Franz Myer, had evaded us. He was the German equivalent of Lawrence of Arabia. If we caught him we would recognise him by a missing finger joint. It took weeks of work and investigation to discover enough about each German to mount an operation to try to catch him.

From Teheran, 16 August 1943:

> I came here thinking it was going to be about the dullest thing imaginable, and feeling that it was just a waste of a keen body, but actually since I returned last from India I have had a most interesting time.

This again is a reference to dealing with the German underground. Something of the flavour of 'mopping up' those Germans can perhaps be conveyed by a brief reference to some particular episodes. The Germans were all armed, and some of them were the toughest of SS Nazi thugs. They were given sanctuary and help by local Persian collaborators.

There was the night when some of us took the two Poles who did guard duty at the PAIFORCE security office in Teheran, and laid on an ambush for some of the German SS parachutists who planned to take some high explosive from Teheran to a new hideout in the country which involved them in using a cross-country track in the foothills of the Elburz mountains just north of Teheran. Although it was necessary for us all to be armed, because we knew that the Germans would be, I gave strict instructions that there was to be no shooting unless the Germans fired first. The plan was to grab the Germans the moment we stopped their vehicle, because we wanted them alive for interrogation.

We laid the ambush in the bottom of a steep little ravine. I stayed on top to give the signal when the German vehicle was approaching.

Eventually I saw the dimmed headlights of a vehicle coming towards me in and out of the little ravines. I gave the signal to block the track with a vehicle.

The ambush went off precisely as planned. We brought the

German vehicle to an abrupt and unexpected halt exactly where we wanted it. But for the Poles, who had lost everything to the Germans in Poland, the only good Germans were dead ones, and they immediately emptied their revolvers into the German vehicle. I managed with difficulty to stop the shooting, and we dragged the shaken Germans out of the car, and a Persian who was in fact our agent. It had been turned into a fire-bucket of bullet holes but, extraordinarily, no one was hit in the dark. I don't like to think what would have happened to all of us if a bullet had gone into the two hundredweight of gelignite in the boot of the car.

Although individual Persians, like the one mentioned in the above paragraph, were prepared to help us, we got no official assistance from the Persian authorities. A freebooting body of people like us could hardly expect official recognition. It was as much as the Persian authorities could do not to frustrate our operations, which were hardly legal.

Our Persian agent who was with the Germans was employed by them and had fixed up a hide for them for their explosives and was taking them to it. He, like the rest of us, accepted that there might be some danger in our ambush arrangements if there was any shooting. He was lucky to survive.

Another very different occasion was when I and one of the PAIFORCE officers spent a night in the labyrinthine Teheran bazaar hunting for a German. We had with us a Teheran prostitute who had been living with him. After moving about and questioning a lot of people during the night, we came at about 7 o'clock in the morning to a dosshouse where he might have spent the night. It was a two-storied house. My colleague took on the ground floor, and I went up and took on the first floor. I opened one door after another and found both men and women in various stages of undress. Then I kicked the door open into a room where I found a man in bed and just reaching for his revolver which was on a shelf beside him. I jammed mine in his face and roared at him in my best German to put his hands up, which he did, very awkwardly, in bed. I told him to get up and get dressed. Then my colleague arrived and we handcuffed the German, who spent the rest of the war in a prisoner of war camp in Syria.

On another occasion we had information that a German was going to a certain house in the evening. I and one of the professors went there in mufti and we found a woman alone in the house. She confirmed that someone was going to visit the house that evening but she did not know who or why.

There were bushes both sides of the gate, and I and the professor waited in them, one each side. At length a man who was obviously a European came in through the gate. We pounced on him and searched him. He was armed and a German, so we handcuffed him and took him back to our headquarters. When we interrogated him, we discovered that a Persian was to go to the lady's house that evening and take him somewhere else. So we went back to the house and waited once more in the bushes.

In due course a Persian arrived dressed in the uniform of a Persian Government Ministry concierge. We could not arrest him, but invited him to come to our headquarters for a talk. He was quite open and said that he had been instructed to take the German to a certain house in Teheran. So we decided to search the house. It was on a corner of a street.

There were five of us, all in mufti and all armed. We knocked on the door which was opened by an elderly Persian servant woman. We pushed her aside and went in and began quickly to search the place. In one room we found a German lying on the floor in a sleeping bag with a pistol by his side.

We addressed him in German to which he responded, so we made him get up and searched him. He had one finger joint missing, so we knew that we had at last captured the elusive German leader, Franz Myer. We laid him out on the floor again with one of the university dons standing guard over him with a very shaky revolver while we searched the house. At one moment the don said to me, 'The German says he is thirsty. Give him a drink from that glass on the chimneypiece, but you had better taste it first to make sure that it isn't poisoned!'

The elderly woman servant took all these proceedings very calmly. She made no protest, said nothing, and seemed quite unconcerned when we took Franz Myer away, as though it was quite an everyday affair for a posse of foreigners to enter your house and kidnap one of the occupants.

I found the capture of Franz Myer rather an anti-climax. I had had no doubt that our procedures were so effective that one day we would get him. That day had arrived. That was all, and he was now a pathetic sight lying on the floor with a wobbly professorial gun held over him. Perhaps it's the hunt that counts, not the kill.

After we had interrogated him he spent the remainder of the war in a prisoner of war camp. His interrogation did not yield anything we had not already learnt from the earlier captives we had made. Franz Myer's method of controlling the other stay-behind Germans was to send for them from time to time (by the use of Persian collaborators such as the one we had intercepted) and discuss their work with them.

Eventually we had caught all the Germans except five: four particularly hardened SS men who had been parachuted into south Persian tribal territory, and a German consul who had gone to ground with the same tribe at the time we invaded Persia, and who was able to act as interpreter for the parachutists. These men were a potential very dangerous threat to the Persian railway that ran from the Persian Gulf to South Russia and which was vital for war supplies to Russia. It was very vulnerable because it ran through the Zagros mountains with numerous bridges over ravines and many tunnels, and could be sabotaged in a variety of places. There was no question of a military operation to get these people. It would have taken a much larger military formation than was available, and even then they could have been hidden somewhere in the mountains. In any case we did not want to antagonise a large and important tribe. It was not till some time later that we managed to make a plan to get them.

I wrote to Maxine at the time:

Not the least interesting part of my time here [in Teheran] has been the team of PAIFORCE people with whom I have been working. It is a real team made up of people from many different walks of life, all of considerable ability, all with burning zeal, so different from one another that they made a complete composite whole. There has never been a touch of friction, and never a trace of pettiness. The whole outfit is characterised by a broad outlook and good humour. And the members of the group were not personally ambitious men. They were, as my experience in Intelligence generally is, too engrossed in what they were doing, in collaboration with like-minded colleagues, to feel a desire to further their own personal advancement. All those in the Teheran Security Office had the ability to achieve higher rank in some other field of activity.

From Teheran, 23 August 1943:

I wonder why George Jenkin asked you to dinner. I don't think they are much given to entertaining. He has too much to do. I suspect the wily old bird wanted to sound you out about me. I have little doubt that my fate will again be in the melting pot before long.

We had a funny scene in the office garden today when Alan Roger's cat went for a dog. She knocked it down. It got up and ran screaming round the garden with the cat after it with all her Persian fur standing on end. She was twice as quick as the dog and got it again and had to be forcibly pulled off it before she killed it. Not bad work considering she has had kittens twice in four months.

Towards the end of September 1943 I was recalled to Delhi for conferences. During the week or so that I was there, there came a shattering blow. Our dear child, Thomas, who had come down from 'the hills' and was with us in Delhi, died; a lovely little soul went out on the east wind, victim of one of India's dread diseases, and we were left bereft. He died at 5 o'clock on the morning of 1 October 1943 and, India being India, we buried him that same afternoon, and with him there went out from our lives the heart and soul of so much that had been our common joy and interest throughout the previous two years.

The fourteenth-century Persian poet, Ibn Yamin, wrote some beautiful lines which it is very hard to render in comparable English – '*Chizi ki raft, raft...*' 'That which is past is gone. Recall it not, for there is no wisdom in suffering the miseries of life all over again.' Not all can find it possible to practise that precept. The grievous, painful and bitter happenings of life will not for everyone so easily retract from the forefront of the mind. How can one practise to forget?

Being parted again almost immediately by the exigencies of war made it harder for Maxine and me to bear. I will say no more about it.

5
Persia – The Last Phase

On my way back to Persia the first letter I wrote to Maxine was from Gwalior where the only two hotels had been taken over by the Government and, as the flying boat to the lake there was a day late, I had to spend the night in the filthy railway station. From Baghdad, 21 October 1943:

> You will probably have heard that I am delayed as I missed my connection. I am stuck here in Baghdad waiting for the next plane to Teheran so I am staying a few days with Chokra. He is in good form and stands up well against the slings and arrows. He lives in a somewhat tumbledown old house on the bank of the River Tigris, but it is quite comfortable. The climate, I think, is foul. It is windy and dusty, and is still a good deal hotter than Delhi is at this time of year.

'Chokra' was Colonel Wood of the Guides, an old friend of Maxine's and mine, who had a senior staff appointment – G 1 Intelligence – at PAIFORCE HQ in Baghdad. 'Chokra' is the Urdu word for a lad. How he came to have that nickname I do not know. Chokra and I naturally talked a good deal of shop, and the General Officer commanding PAIFORCE asked me to have a talk abut Persia with him, but otherwise I had no work to do in Baghdad.

> Chokra is very kind to me. Tomorrow he is taking me out shooting with a local notable. [The son of General Nuri-es-Said Pasha, the Prime Minister. Both father and son were murdered in a subsequent military coup.] I haven't fired a shot for five years, and I have long since lost my interest in

slaying things. Buddha said, 'Life is dear to all. When a man considers this he does not kill or cause to kill', but the day will do me good, and it is very kind of old Chokra to lay it on.

This is a fairly noisy place at night. There is a continual distant howling of dogs, varied occasionally by piercing yells when someone lands one of them a kick – or threatens to do so. Outside my window is a gas-engine pumping water. Fortunately it hasn't got a whistle on it. It did not start work till about 5.30 a.m. this morning. Just below the window there is chained a neurotic dog. About every ten minutes, when his nerve gives out, he breaks into a high-pitched, hysterical barking in an attempt to revive some courage. Will it be murder when I empty a bucket of water on him? For he will surely die of fright.

From Baghdad, 23 October 1943:

I had my day's shooting yesterday with Chokra and his pals. It was more of a party than a shooting party. We were due to start at 8.45 but some of the party found it hard to stir themselves, and it was somewhere about 11 o'clock before we got moving. We then had an hour's drive to the country estate of Chokra's friend. When we got there, it was discovered that the guns were in one car and the cartridges in a second, which did not turn up till an hour later. So there was no shooting before lunch, but there was a good lot of drinking and card-playing, and a gramophone howled. This quite suited me as I was more interested in the people than the shooting; and, as I was not distracted by the drink or the cards, and had no interest in the gramophone beyond a desire to throw a rock at it, I had some chance for observation. The party consisted altogether of fourteen Iraqis, three of them women, and all dressed in European clothes.

Lunch was a substantial sit-down affair, sitting on the ground. The local *pièce de résistance* is a dish called *kouzeh* which is a roast lamb – whole – stuffed with rice, served on a huge copper tray. Two were provided. Despite the fact that appetites were hearty, half one would have been more than sufficient, particularly as there was much other food besides.

After the meal there was more card playing and gramophoning and, at length, some shooting. We did quite a bit of walking; the standard of shooting was fairly high, and we got quite a few black partridge. We eventually got back soon after dark.

I then went with Chokra to a dinner party at the house of a local Iraqi general. There were some interesting people at it, including two cabinet ministers.

From Baghdad, 25 October 1943:

Yesterday Chokra and a man on his staff who is an archaeologist took me to a place called Korigalzu, which dates back to the fifteenth century BC, where digging is now going on.

They are digging out the remains of a temple and surrounding buildings which were all built of mud brick cemented together with bitumen. Quite a lot of the walls and floors are still intact and there are cuneiform inscriptions on some of the bricks, and on a few stone beds they have found door posts. The civilisation was of Persian origin. The most noticeable thing of interest is a huge brick tower about 150 feet high. They were mountain people and were used to the idea that their gods inhabited the mountain peaks, so when they came and settled here in the plains, there was no reasonable place for the gods so they built this brick mountain for them.

We had a picnic in the open air and a pleasant day. At one place we saw vast flocks of sand grouse. They were in quantities such as I have never seen in India.

On the whole I have had an interesting time here and it has been good for me. Chokra has been most exceedingly kind. He has a very soft corner of his heart for you and has asked kindly after you. I think I told you that he told a lady

[73]

in Teheran that his only interest in going back to India would be to see you again.

On Saturday he took me to the Baghdad races. As they were short of stewards, they asked me to be an honorary steward for the afternoon which I was glad to accept as it gave me something to do. The course is awful, being all dust, but the racing was very interesting.

From Teheran, 27 October 1943, to Maxine:

Here I am pounding the old machine again. As I lent it to the staff while I was away, it has two noticeable features: it is clean, and the ribbon is worn out.

We now have a dog here, a golden cocker puppy aged six months. He really is a charming little chap. His big idea is to play with either a duck on our little pond or a cat. He is trained to live at peace with cats, but our two don't know that yet, so they are horribly rude when he makes advances to them. The ducks also entirely fail to appreciate his attentions; a pity, as the more a flapping, quacking duck flaps and quacks, the more desirable a plaything it becomes for a six-month-old puppy.

Our ducks are now simply magnificent. The drake is in full plumage, a real drake mallard and he is most decorative.

Alan Roger's cat is making arrangements for her third litter since last April. At present she spends most of her time on the roof love-making. The husband is a villainous-looking white brute. They seem to suffer from 'incompatibility' as they are most of the time using the most vile language to each other

The weather has been cold and wet, and cloudy and raw, and miserable. That sounds pretty bad. However, yesterday the sun came out and the mountains sparkled in their fresh covering of snow and it was really lovely. Today it is the same, so I hope we are in for a spell of fine weather now. Last night we had our first frost. Only just a touch on the wet places, but it will get progressively colder now.

I wonder how much longer the Germans are going to stand this bombing. This 2,500-ton raid must have been frightful, and it is going to get a lot worse, I suppose. It is quite impossible to imagine what a raid like that must be like. Think of the damage that 2,500 tons of rocks would do if you dropped them on a city, let alone that weight of the most devastating explosives and incendiaries science can produce.

At the end of November 1943, one of the major conferences of the war was held in Teheran attended by Winston Churchill, British Prime Minister, President Roosevelt of America, and the Russian leader, Joseph Stalin. A letter from me made reference to this, and particularly to the occasion of a birthday dinner for Churchill on 30 November which was held in the British Legation:

The Minister here, Sir Reader Bullard, has just been awarded the KCB. He tells a very amusing story about how it was given to him. At the end of the conference, Churchill said that he would like a plaque put up in the dining room of the Legation to commemorate his historic birthday dinner to which the other two leaders were invited.

He then said that he proposed to recommend to the King that he make Sir Reader a KCB. Sir Reader objected, saying that he had had absolutely nothing to do with the conference and that it was just by chance that he happened to be the Minister here when it took place. Churchill said, 'Never mind. It was a historic occasion.' Sir Reader then said he would accept it, but he added, 'What it amounts to is that you want to put a plaque on me as well as on the dining room.' Churchill said, 'That's right. We're going to put a plaque on you too.'

Christmas Day 1943, to Maxine:

I got out of hospital, where I have been with 'flu, fever, etc. for some days, just in time for the Christmas festivities. I am much better.

When in hospital I read Dr Johnson to the finish, a thing I have never done before. There isn't a dull page in it, but one needs to be in bed to get through the 600-odd pages.

26 December 1943:

Well, I think and hope Christmas is now over for me. We had our little party here last night, and a Christmas tree! I have not over-eaten or over-drunk, and am suffering from nothing worse than having been out of bed till 1 a.m. last night, so I guess I'm pretty lucky. I think that by Christmas 1945 we shall have peace everywhere, but I don't think we need expect it earlier.

I often wonder what we should have done had we been subjected to what many of these poor Poles here have been through. Torn from their homes, families divided, some dead, some missing, only the strongest surviving, they find themselves in some strange land. At the best, though many of them probably came from good and comfortable homes, they can now expect some form of indigent, communal camp life. And God knows what agonies of worry they may suffer, mothers parted from their children, wives parted from their husbands; years of suspense not knowing who is alive and who is dead, and not knowing whether indeed they shall ever know the fate of their nearest relations.

You will be pleased to hear that I wore the new socks on Christmas Day. I have always been lucky to be associated with good sock-makers. I think you are very high class, and the socks are both comfortable and smart.

We seem to have had a good war week, what with naval successes, very heavy bombing, and this new huge Russian offensive, which looks like finally smashing up the German front in Russia.

From Teheran, 9 January 1944:

We are in the midst of the Muharram, and today is the Ruz-i-Qatl, or the day on which the slaughter of Hussain, the founder of the Shias, by the Sunnis is commemorated. The late Shah put an end to the celebrations in this country. In old days not only did fanatical Shias parade themselves through the streets beating themselves with chains and slashing themselves with razors as a sign of lamentation, but they also took the opportunity to slaughter the rival Sunnis who are in the minority in Persia. They are no longer allowed to molest Sunnis, but they have resumed the beating and slashing.

I lunched with the Frasers yesterday. Mrs Fraser has been in bed with pneumonia, but the same military doctor who looked after me gave her M & B 693 [a new wonder drug at that time] which cured her in a week. M & B certainly seems to have got the measure of pneumonia.

General Fraser was in great heart. [He was my old CO W.A.K. Fraser, who was now British Military Attaché in Teheran.] He seems to be better than he has been for years. He said he was out for a walk last week on the Ruz-i-Qatl when he saw a little girl by the side of the road in floods of tears. He asked her what she was crying about, and she replied that she had no *chadur-nashin* (veil) and so could not go with the other girls to the mosque. There, of course, everyone was having a whale of a time howling their heads off and weeping their eyes out in memory of the martyrdom of the blessed Hussain. General Fraser asked her how much it would cost her to get a veil, and she said five toumans. So he gave her the money, whereupon she stopped crying and, after a moment's thought, said, 'I think I'll buy myself a pair of stockings with this. If you'll give me another five I'll get the veil.'

20 January 1944:

As I have been somewhat neglected by Delhi, I have written to George to ask him if he can give me any idea what it is proposed to do with me in the future as I suspect that there will not be much more for me to do here. I have told him that I want to return to combat soldiering and that I am prepared to accept a reduction in rank and appointment to facilitate this. One never knows quite what course of action is right, but I feel that I have done what seems best and anyway, if it comes to anything, I shall be satisfied.

I am very sorry to hear about Hume Jones. I had known him all my service. He was very steady, sound and able and quite one of the best of my contemporaries in the Army. He will be much missed.

Hume Jones had started in the King's Shropshire Light Infantry (KSLI) and then transferred to the Indian Army (13th Frontier Force Rifles). He was one of the most able soldiers in the Army, besides being an exceptionally nice, modest and friendly man. Had he survived, he could hardly have failed to go to the top. His brother, 'Splosh' Jones, who became a full general (General Sir Charles Jones), told me that he would be the first to acknowledge that Hume was a much more able man than himself.

23 February 1944, to Maxine:

I agree partly, in principle, with what you said in your letter written in the train about me being more useful doing something at which I am experienced. Actually, I made this point to George when I wrote to him. I think that from now on (or rather from this time last year when we seized the initiative) everything else should be cut to the bone to provide men to fight. We have the material; we have the initiative. The more trained men we have for fighting, and the sooner we throw them against the enemy, the quicker the war is going to be won. The very winning of victories will solve many secondary problems on which we may now be concentrating too much of our energy. I felt this a year ago. I don't feel it any less now. There should be a real comb out of all other services to find fighting men. If that was done I, for one, as a regular soldier, would be back at regimental duty which, despite some opinion to the contrary, is where I could be of most use and, on the whole, that for which I am best trained. However, I agree that, with things as they are, the chances are that it might be considered that I would be better elsewhere.

At the end of February 1944 I was back in my old haunts in the tribal area of south Persia where I had spent a year in 1935/36, and where the four German SS parachutists and Consul Schultz were still in the mountains and a potential menace to the vulnerable south/north railway through the Zagros mountains.

The Teheran security people had not been able to do anything about these Germans. I therefore decided to ask the British Minister, Sir Reader Bullard, if I could have a go at trying to persuade the tribe to hand them over to us. I had spent a year in that tribe's area, when I was studying Persian. Both Sir Reader Bullard and the Military Attaché, General W.A.K. Fraser, thought it would be useless because of tribal rules of hospitality, but they agreed to my going and having a shot at it.

As soon as I got to the area, I made contact with old Persian friends and tried to get an introduction to the tribal leaders. After some days I was called on by a man who said he would take me to the tribe if I would go with him. I did not know whether this was a trap but decided to go nevertheless. The tribe were out in the mountains, but he took me to a commodious house on the outskirts of the town where I was staying. He went in and took me up to the first floor and into a large room furnished as a Persian sitting room, and introduced me to a Persian lady, Bibi Khanum. She was middle-aged, tall for a Persian woman, stately and aristocratic, and very well dressed. She was the mother of the tribal leader, but I was to come to realise that she, and not he, ruled the tribe. She had with her a sharp foxy-looking man who was her confidential secretary. I felt as though I was meeting Queen Elizabeth I and Will Cecil.

I spent three weeks arguing with those two in Persian until they then capitulated, and Bibi Khanum said that I must go into

[79]

the mountains to see Nasser Khan, the tribal leader, who would arrange to hand over the Germans to me. Again I was not sure whether or not this was a trap, but concluded that I was not going to get any further if I did not put myself into the hands of the tribe. So out into the mountains I went, escorted by tribesmen. There I had lunch with the tribal leader and other senior tribesmen. We sat on the ground on Persian carpets and ate a roast lamb and, after lunch, the tribal leader took me aside and told me that the Germans would be handed over to me at 8.30 a.m. on a certain date at a place named Mian-i-Shah near the town of Abade, 100 miles north of where we were, but he would not tell me where Mian-i-Shah was. I sent a coded message from our local consulate to Teheran, telling them to be at a certain place on the road at the appointed time with a large enough escort for the job. I then went to the town of Abade and put up in the caravanserai there. I found that the local Persian Governor was an old friend from my student days when I had known him and his wife well. I called on them and they invited me to supper. I asked him if he still went shooting. He did, and invited me to shoot and lent me a gun. That was just what I wanted as I hoped it would give me a chance to find out where Mian-i-Shah was.

At one point in the shoot we climbed up a ridge and looked down into a valley in the middle of which was a crumbling mud fort. I asked where it was and was told that it was a place named Mian-i-Shah. That was all I wanted to know.

At the appointed time and place the Germans were there inside the mud fort with their tribal escort. Our party of people, which consisted of four members of our Teheran Security Office and two Red Caps (military policemen) had already arrived from Teheran and we took custody of the Germans. It was perhaps something of an achievement to have persuaded the main tribe to give up the Germans, thus breaching the code of tribal hospitality, but they saved their honour by the fact that the Germans were not handed over to us by the main tribe but by a lesser tribe. They had been relieved of their money, explosives and arms. The four parachutists were dreadful thugs, but the German consul, Bertholt Schultz, was different. I said to him, 'These chaps are going back to Teheran handcuffed in the back of an open army truck; 500 miles of dirt road and dust and acute discomfort. You are a member of your diplomatic corps and a gentleman. If you will give your word that you will not try any funny business I will take you in my station wagon. It is uncomfortable enough but a good deal better than the back of an open truck.' He agreed and, after the war, he wrote a book in German about his Persian experiences, *Daybreak over Iran*. He referred to this incident. He did not know my name but paid me the compliment of calling me 'the courteous major'.

The four SS Nazi thugs were bitter at being captured and said that, even if we won this war, there would be another, and next time they would be sure of winning. One of them, a fanatical Nazi, had a razor blade hidden in the sole of his boot and managed to sever his wrist after he had been taken into custody in Teheran. He was taken to hospital where he jumped out of a fifth storey lavatory window, and the world was one Nazi less.

While I was on this mission to south Persia there were some nice and interesting moments:

I visited Persepolis and had a walk round the ruins. They have done a lot of work on them since I was there in 1935. Much of the carving which has been recently excavated is not going to last. I talked to a foreman – who was the only person I could find – who told me that the rock, after having been buried for 2,000 years or more, appears after being exposed to suffer from sunburn. At any rate the beautiful grey stone of a staircase, which had just been excavated when I was here last, has vanished. The rock now looks rusty, and the outer surface, in which the bas reliefs are carved, is peeling off like flakes of slate. They are putting up shades now to keep the sun off, but the damage is done.

One evening I was taken out to a marsh by some shooters. I, fortunately, did not have to shoot. I don't feel any desire to do so again. It was a Peter Scott evening. A big plain surrounded by mountains of every shade of pink, mauve, purple and blue, with a big flash of water in it several square miles in extent covered with waterfowl. When someone fired a shot some seven or eight hundred wild geese rose with a roar of wings from the water and, forming themselves into long skeins, winged their way into the sunset till their cries could be heard no more. Thousands of duck too were soon in the air. I remembered this place when I was here before, but I never saw this quantity of wildfowl on it. Can it be that five years of war have given the ducks and geese a chance to multiply their numbers vastly? An adjutant stork came and sat down quite close to me. He picked up a frog which, when he raised his head, slid like a flash down his long beak into his mouth. But he flew away before I could take a photo of him. The East is at its best when the sun is sinking on a fresh, still evening across a flash of water where the cries of the wild birds mingle with the distant sound of camel bells. Those, perhaps, are the things that I shall remember when I am old and warming my lumbago before the fire on a bleak winter's night at home, when the wind is moaning in the chimney and rattling the windows.

I have been places where I had not been before. I had a fascinating trip into the wilder parts where spring was in full bloom and the mountain sides were covered with wild almond in blossom. I have been somewhat overwhelmed with hospitality, and one old Persian friend has given me a volume of Hafiz – one of Persia's most celebrated poets – which I am never likely to read as I doubt that I shall ever have either the time or the inclination to revive my Persian sufficiently. It was in Shiraz that Hafiz lived and it would probably not be wrong to say that Hafiz, and not the Koran, contains the religion of the educated Shirazi. Sa'adi also was a Shirazi and is buried a mile or so from the grave of Hafiz. They have restored the grave of Hafiz since I was here and it is now quite imposing. I love Sa'adi above all the poets.

Having finally mopped up the last of the German underground organisation in Persia, I wrote to Maxine:

As you will know by now, I am for pastures new – or old. I shall be leaving here in about a week and probably reaching Delhi round about ten days to a fortnight later, so this is possibly the last letter I shall send you from here. I shall be very sorry to say goodbye to the friends with whom I have worked so closely through such interesting times here, but it is time for me to go. It is also satisfactory that the high interest [of mopping up the German underground agents] has been sustained to the very end.

I returned to India from Persia early in April 1944. The war with Germany had a little more than another year to run; the war with Japan ended three months after the end of the war with Germany. I reckoned that I had done my stint of unorthodox soldiering and I hoped that that would be recognised and that I would now be allowed to return to an orthodox command of troops in the field.

Immediately on my return to Delhi, therefore, I called on those concerned to ask if a decision had been taken about my future. I was assured that very careful consideration had been given to it. It was fully appreciated, I was told, that I would like to get back to a field command of troops, but the fact was that there was no shortage of people with the training, experience and ability to do that, whereas I had particular experience, knowledge and aptitude wherewith it was judged that I could make a more fruitful contribution to the war effort 'doing other things'. The consequence was that I spent the remainder of the war 'doing other things'. Perhaps they were right. Churchill in *The Second World War* volume 2, *Their Finest Hour*, page 19, wrote: 'Displacements in a sphere so intimate and so concerned with secret matters are detrimental to continuous and efficient despatch of business.'

The appointment, the 'other things' that had been decided upon for me between the Director of the Intelligence Bureau and the Commander-in-Chief, was to run the Silver double agent case together with one of the Intelligence Bureau officers, Malcolm Johnston.

This double agent work was also practised on a wide scale and most successfully in England and the Middle East. Its most significant triumph was related to D Day in Europe. Those who were running the double agent cases in England persuaded the Germans that the attack on Europe might be launched in Norway, the Low Countries or the Pas de Calais area of France, causing the Germans to tie up forces there while the landings were actually taking place in Normandy.

Three months after the end of the war with Japan Maxine and I had an occasion for domestic rejoicing. Another son, George, was born to us and he has proved a great credit to the family as he is now a leading London banker – and Maxine had the enormous pleasure and satisfaction of once more having a baby to look after. On the night that he was born Vera Cumming, the wife of one of my brother officers, and I played duets on the piano to keep our nerves under control. Perhaps that is why George is so musical.

With the end of the war, Maxine's father had decided to retire. That meant closing his large house in Delhi, where she had been living with him, and it was decided that both she and he would go home to England sometime in the early part of 1946. She, in the event, went some weeks before he did, with her baby.

I had been given a staff appointment in Delhi, both clearing up after the war and making preparations to meet the acute problems that were facing us in India. The old order had changed. The wonderful life in India as we had known it pre-war had largely seeped away, and was clearly on the threshold of total extinction.

While Malcolm Johnston and I were running the Silver case Dick White, the then Director of Intelligence in MI5, paid a visit to India and had a long talk with us about the Silver case and other Intelligence matters. The upshot for us was that at a later date we were both invited to join MI5. Malcolm went to the Far East as Head of SIFE (Security Intelligence Far East). He hated flying but he set off one morning, together with the Far East Director of Military Intelligence, to fly to Hong Kong. They were never heard of again and no aircraft wreckage was ever found.

6
Palestine

The last phase of my Indian Army career was now about to begin. Early in 1946, the year following the end of the war, I was told that MI5 – on the prompting of Dick White, no doubt – had asked for me on secondment to take over their operation in Palestine where the Jewish rebellion was in full swing. This information was given to me by George Jenkin, deputy director of the Indian Intelligence Bureau, whose judgement I much respected, and the man with his finger most surely on the pulse of Indian Intelligence affairs. I told him that I had doubts about accepting the Palestine job. I was in no doubt that we were going to be faced with acute difficulties in India and, as a member of the Indian services, I thought that that was where my primary duty lay. I felt I ought to remain in India. He said he thought I should accept the Palestine job, saying, 'They've got an acute problem there already. Ours here may be some way off.' So I accepted.

I was not wanted in Palestine until September 1946, when the man *en poste* was due to leave; but I was required to spend some weeks at the Headquarters of MI5 in London first for 'familiarisation'. I also wanted a few weeks' leave. I had had none, except for the occasional week now and again, for the past seven years. I therefore left India in the spring of 1946, and went home for the third time in seventeen years. Though I remained a member of the Indian Army and continued to wear my Hodson's Horse uniform, I did not serve again in India. I was, from then on, working *de facto* for MI5.

I duly arrived in Palestine in September 1946, shortly after the military headquarters in the King David Hotel had been bombed with appalling loss of innocent life and a dreadful toll of injury to British personnel. Five people on my staff were killed. Ninety-six people all told lost their lives.

Palestine meant separation again from Maxine, as wives and families were not allowed there for security reasons. While I was there, our third son, Hugh, was born in December 1946. I was not able to attend his christening, but sent home a small flask of Jordan water for the occasion.

I lived in the senior officers' mess in Jerusalem. The messing was awful, so I offered to act as mess secretary and was able to make some improvements. Although a teetotaller myself, I was concerned to try to get decent wine for the mess at a reasonable price, and discovered that the Trappist monastery at Latrun at the west foot of the Judean hills made very good wine at manageable cost. I visited the monastery two or three times. Brother Thomas, the only brother allowed to talk, was very welcoming and pleasant and showed me round the monastery and the grounds. The fine buildings had all been built by the monks themselves. However, I am afraid that the atmosphere of those men going about their affairs in perpetual silence was to me very uncongenial.

No one brought up on the Bible could have thought it other than a privilege to serve in Palestine, and be able to see on the ground places familiar in the Bible stories. Who could see the River Jordan without thinking of Christ being baptised there by John? Or without recalling Naaman, the Syrian general, 'a mighty man of valour' who, in a very human story, was persuaded by his batman to swallow his pride and wash in the miserable little River Jordan to cleanse him of his leprosy, rather than bathe in Abana and Pharpar, the prestigious rivers of Syria?

Or who could visit Nablus without recalling the story of the Woman of Samaria, and Jacob's well: 'Jesus, being wearied, sat on the well.' That used to intrigue me. How could he sit on the well? But, in fact, it proves today to be a convenient place to sit. It has a low parapet wall around it just the right height, and I am prepared to suppose that it was similar 2,000 years ago.

And during the conversation the woman said to Jesus, 'Our fathers worshipped in this mountain' and there, as you sit on the well, is the mountain opposite you, with a shrine high up on its shoulder.

And I liked to think of old Elijah, by the brook Kerith, being fed by the ravens – or had the story become inverted and was he, like me in the High Himalayas, giving tit-bits to some friendly and inquisitive ravens? Indeed, around every corner in what was Palestine is a familiar Bible story.

The subject of Palestine, the emergence of Israel, the Palestine Liberation Organisation, the Occupied Territories, American influence, Syrian influence, the reduction by external influence of the one democratic country in the Middle East, Lebanon, to chaos, and other associated issues, are still ongoing matters of great international complexity. Nevertheless, even the most disagreeable situations – and Palestine in 1946/47 was hardly an agreeable one – can leave room for some pleasant things, not the least of which in Palestine was working with respected, able and cherished colleagues, in particular our GOC, Major General 'Babe' MacMillan (later General Sir Gordon MacMillan), the mildest of men but a tiger of a soldier.

Psalm 137 begins 'By the waters of Babylon we [the Jews] sat down and wept: when we remembered thee, O Zion.' Zion is Palestine, or more specifically Jerusalem. Although the Jewish people had taken Palestine from the Canaanites, they thereafter always regarded it as their homeland. Palestine was frequently involved in Middle East wars and conflicts, and there were two occasions when the Palestinian Jews were themselves overrun and exiled. The first was when King Nebuchadnezzar destroyed Jerusalem and carried off the Jews into captivity in Babylon in 587 BC. The second was the rebellion against Rome in AD 132, led by Simon Bar Kochba, when Jerusalem was lost to them again and there was another dispersal of the Jewish people. These dispersals came to be called the Diaspora. The majority of Jews settled down abroad, but there was throughout the centuries a strong current of anti-Semitism wherever Jews had settled, and in the nineteenth century this led to a sizeable minority who in the words of the Psalms 'remembered thee, O Zion' and longed for Palestine to become the Jewish homeland once more.

Towards the end of the nineteenth century the so-called Zionist movement became politically very active under the leadership of Theodor Herzl, and directed itself, particularly in response to Russian pogroms, to establishing a Zionist political state. It was suggested that this might be in East Africa but, for the East European Jews in particular, nothing would do but to have the Jewish state in Palestine. This movement did not achieve much for the next fifty years or so, and up to the early 1930s the Jews were in a minority in Palestine.

At the beginning of the First World War Palestine was a part of the Turkish Empire. In that war Turkey was part of the enemy alliance and it fell to the British to fight the Turks in Palestine. In 1917 Jerusalem was captured by a British force commanded by General Sir Edmund (later Field Marshal Viscount) Allenby, and in 1919 Palestine was placed under British governance as a mandated territory from the United Nations.

In 1917, to curry favour with, and to gain the support of, Jews everywhere, the British Foreign Secretary, Balfour, addressed a letter to a leading British Jew, Lord Rothschild, stating British support for the establishment in Palestine of a national home for the Jewish people on the understanding that 'nothing shall be done which may prejudice the civil and religious rights of existing non-Jewish communities in Palestine'.

The Balfour Declaration was rejected by both Muslims and Christian Arabs and in the early 1920s there were a number of Arab anti-Zionist revolts, even though the British administration had put a quota (16,500) on the number of Jews who would be permitted to settle annually in Palestine. The problem became acute when the Nazis came to power in Germany and began to persecute the Jews, prompting an exodus eager to flee from Germany and to settle in Palestine. In 1936 the Arabs, seriously perturbed by the pressure of Jewish immigration, staged a serious revolt against the British mandatory Government in Palestine. Casualties were high: 5,000 Arabs killed and wounded, more than 1,000 Jews and 500 British casualties.

In 1939 the quota of Jewish immigrants was raised to 75,000 and later an additional 1,500 were allowed in monthly. It became clear and was accepted by the British Government that the Jewish aim was to parcel off a part of Palestine into a Jewish state, and that the British mandate should be terminated. But what is liable to happen in such conditions of political manoeuvring is that an extreme minority take up arms to try to secure by force what is evolving too slowly for them by political dialogue.

The Palestine situation at that time threw up three such organisations: the Stern Gang, the Irgun Zvai Leumi and the Hagenah. The Irgun Zvai Leumi was a classic terrorist organisation devoted to the murder of British personnel and the destruction of vital parts of the British infrastructure. The Stern Gang was an even more zealous splinter group which broke off from the Irgun Zvai Leumi. The Hagenah was the future army of the coming Jewish state in embryo, but it had its links with the terrorist organisations and was involved in some terrorist activity.

These were the principal organisations whose activities, plans, targets and so on my office in Palestine, working very closely with the exceedingly efficient Palestine Police Special Branch, was concerned to cover. There was in addition a major illegal immigration problem on which my office was able to supply information vital to the Palestine Government. This was the flow of ships from Europe carrying thousands of illegal immigrants to Palestine. Although their missions were carried out with great secrecy by the Jewish organisation controlling them, the vital information which we were able to provide resulted in the interception of most of the ships. Their cargoes of immigrants were temporarily interned in Cyprus.

There was in Palestine at that time a committee of senior

Jewish officials known as the Jewish Agency. They were the Jewish Government in waiting, poised for the moment when the Jews might be able to seize some of the Palestine territory. I knew them all and was indeed on almost friendly terms with them even though I must have been high on the Jewish target list.

I told them that I though they were making a grave mistake trying to set up a home for the Jews – indeed a Jewish state – in Palestine. I said, 'You may pack a couple of million Jews into your little Jewish state, but you will for ever more be surrounded by two hundred million Muslims who will never leave you alone.'

In December 1946, three months after I had gone to Palestine, I was ordered to go to General Headquarters, Middle East Land Forces (GHQ, MELF) in Cairo, to take temporary charge, until the permanent incumbent came out from England, of the Department directing MI5 work throughout the Middle East. This included the work for which I was responsible in Palestine. Its title was 'Security Intelligence Middle East' (SIME).

Accommodation was difficult in Cairo but I found myself a bed-sitting room in the spacious flat of an elderly Austrian lady, a widow. With her lived her daughter, also a widow, who had been married to a Turkish officer, and in the flat too was the daughter's nineteen-year-old son, who was shortly going to the United States to study engineering. I spoke to him one day about his remarkable knowledge of languages. Because his grandmother preferred to talk German, he and his mother always spoke to her in German. Because his father had been a Turk, he spoke Turkish. Educated at English schools in Egypt, he spoke English, and because French was the language of polite society in Cairo, he spoke French. Having been born and bred in Egypt, he spoke Arabic and, because he had been brought up in Alexandria where there are large Greek and Italian populations, he spoke Greek and Italian.

I remarked how wonderful it must be to have command of all those languages.

'It's hell,' he replied. 'I have no mother tongue. I never know in what language to think.'

After a few weeks in Cairo I handed over to the new permanent incumbent and went home for a conference in London. On my return to Palestine, I wrote:

I have been very busy and indeed today is the first day that I have taken any time off at all. However, we are slowly getting things straightened out here and I hope soon we shall be leading a more normal existence. The disturbed state of the country and all the restrictions don't add to the joys of life.

It has been an exceptionally mild winter here, and is now quite warm. Unfortunately the winter rains almost completely failed and this has caused great loss and hardship, particularly to the Arabs in the southern part of the country. I went out of Jerusalem today for the first time since I got back, and did a trip to Gaza via Hebron and Beersheba. The rolling plain around Beersheba, which at this time of year should be a sea of young corn, is little more than a desert. In the Judean hills things were better and the wild flowers were lovely.

When I came out from England this time I was in distinguished company and flew in one of the two York aircraft which they keep for Cabinet Ministers and senior people. It was the same aircraft which took Monty to Moscow.

We left Cambridge just as it was getting dark. We were delayed starting because, just before we were due to go, two of the crew said they were not feeling well. The doctor found they had jaundice; they had been in Rangoon a week or two before and he thought they might have contracted it there. So a couple of spares were called up and an extra pilot was thrown in for luck in case the two pilots, who had also been to Rangoon, developed jaundice too; and we started.

It was like taking off from the North Pole as the whole country was thick under snow. We then had a tremendous flight all night without coming down, and landed next morning at Fayid on the Suez Canal in nice time for break-fast. [GHQ, MELF had moved from Cairo to Fayid on the shores of the Great Bitter Lake through which the Suez Canal runs.]

I spent the day there working in GHQ. The next morning we were to come on to Palestine. We had three shots at get-ting the York aircraft off the ground, but it wouldn't take off. By that time we had set the brakes on fire so we had to abandon it. However, the RAF lent us another plane and we got to Palestine without further incident. I was very glad to be back as this country really fascinates me, and I hope they will now leave me here.

7
Transjordan

I took three days off at Easter and went with one of my officers, Harry Duncan, to Transjordan. The weather was perfect
and we had a very pleasant little holiday. Going down by
Jericho, we crossed the Jordan at Allenby Bridge and then
went on until we were within ten miles or so of Amman
when we took a track to the north for some twenty miles to
Jerash. I wrote:

> The country is mostly an open, undulating hilly country
> between 2,000 and 4,000 feet above sea level, in places
> wooded. The soil is for the most part a deep red colour and,
> with a patchwork of young green crops covering the hills, it
> was very colourful against the clear blue sky. I had my paint-
> box with me but never found an opportunity to paint.
> Jerash is really a fascinating place. It was one of the ten
> Greek cities of the Decapolis. Amman, the present capital of
> Transjordan, is another, and was the old Philadelphia. Prob-
> ably there was a city at Jerash in pre-Greek times, but it was
> the Greeks who founded the magnificent town whose ruins
> are there now. The Romans added to it. There is a fine gate-
> way built by Hadrian (the builder of 'the Wall' between Eng-
> land and Scotland in AD 122) who came to Palestine from
> Britain. He too was responsible for the final elimination of
> the Jews in Palestine and Transjordan, 580,000 of them
> being slaughtered at the time. In post-Roman times there
> were probably further additions to Jerash, and the place
> appears to have been inhabited until about the ninth century
> AD when it was destroyed by an earthquake. Thereafter it
> declined and was finally abandoned, to be altogether lost

and forgotten for six or seven hundred years until it was rediscovered about a century and a half ago.

The central existing feature of the city is a paved street about a mile long with colonnades down either side. Some of the columns are still standing. At the southern end of the street is a beautiful colonnaded forum or circus, about 100 yards in diameter, paved in a more or less concentric pattern.

An underground drainage system runs under the street. Halfway along the street are the remains of what must have been a really lovely multiple fountain. The ruts worn in the paving by the vehicles or chariots are still to be seen. There are many fine buildings, including two theatres with excellent acoustics. Even the numbers on the seats are still visible. You can really sit in the theatre and reconstruct in your mind the scenes of 2,000-odd years ago.

In recent years the Turks imported Circassians into Transjordan, and there is now a Circassian village just across the valley from Jerash.

The Circassians had originated from Circassia in the Caucasus region of what was South Russia. They are noted for their striking physical beauty.

The Turkish Empire had ruled over these lands for 600 years before it was defeated and destroyed in the First World War. The Circassians had unfortunately quarried ancient Jerash buildings to obtain building materials for their own village dwellings.

I wrote:

We went into Amman for the night. Having failed to get a room in a hotel we slept in our office there and fed in the hotel which is a friendly, expensive, semi-modern affair and none too clean.

On the following day we took a track to the south for twenty miles or so along the tops of the mountains of Moab. Our vehicle was a Jeep. The mountains of Moab are not really mountains. They are an undulating plateau some

3,000 feet above sea level, but the great rift of the Jordan valley and the Dead Sea (into which there is a precipitous drop of 4,000 feet) gives them the appearance of mountains from the west. [The Dead Sea is 1,300 feet below sea level. It is also 1,300 feet deep, which gives the measure of this rift in the earth's crust.]

The country appeared to be virtually uninhabited though much of it was covered with young green crops, presumably sown by nomads. It was therefore surprising to come upon the little town of Madaba. It is built of stone on a little hill, and looks like something transplanted from Europe. We did not go into it. The centre of it, on the summit of the hill, appeared to be a large monastery; on the outskirts were two new apparently Roman Catholic churches. The people were the usual mixture so common in this area. You cease to be surprised at Arab children with fair hair and blue eyes. In one family some are dark and others fair. I suppose they contain the blood of Greeks, Romans, Persians, Assyrians, Crusaders, desert Arabs, Turks, Egyptians, African slaves, to say nothing of Australians and Cockneys.

Skirting Madaba we took a very rough track for a few miles north east, and eventually halted on Mount Nebo and ate our lunch at the spot where Moses is supposed to have had his only view of the Promised Land. It is a fine view but not very promising. 4,000 feet below are the blue waters of the Dead Sea and, beyond, the mountains of Judea, with the spires of two buildings on the Mount of Olives just visible against the skyline if you have good eyes. Stretching away to the north is the burnt and desert Jordan valley, looking very hot and uninviting.

We spent most of the day lazing in the sun and it was very pleasant. Nearby we found some black irises. I have never seen them before and think they must be rare.

The next day we wandered about the ancient ruins in Amman and then came slowly home, spending a couple of hours in the shade of a mulberry tree by the roadside where we lunched. There we saw a chameleon. He was wonderfully camouflaged against the green of the tree. Harry Duncan caught him in his handkerchief. He didn't like that and turned a sickly yellow colour.

Although Harry and I were having a holiday, we inspected our office in Amman and discussed local security problems, including the inevitable effect on Transjordan of the establishment of a Jewish state in Palestine.

8

The Middle East

As things turned out I was not destined to stay much longer in
Palestine. The health of the new Head of SIME broke down
after six months. He had a nervous breakdown from overwork.
He was invalided home. I was promoted to brigadier and
ordered to Egypt to take over as Head of SIME (Security Intelligence Middle East). When I got there I went to live in the
senior officers' mess in Fayid. Married families were allowed
there, but accommodation was very short and, despite all my
efforts to get a married quarter, it was more than another year
before Maxine and our two sons could join me. My predeces-
sor had been a bachelor so that I was not in a position to inherit
any married accommodation.

SIME was an inter-service organisation – Army, Navy and
Air Force personnel plus some MI5 clerical staff. It took its
Intelligence direction from MI5. The overall responsibility of
MI5 was 'The Defence of the Realm as a whole from Espi-
onage, Subversion and Sabotage'. The whole of the Middle
East area, being of vital interest to British imperial strategy at
that time, came within the terms of 'The Realm as a whole'.

I was not only responsible to MI5, but also to all British
authorities in the area for their security needs and interests. The
authorities in question were: the Army Commander-in-Chief
Middle East; the Naval Commander-in-Chief Mediterranean;
the Royal Air Force Commander-in-Chief Middle East; the
Naval Commander-in-Chief Eastern Fleet (whose area of
responsibility included the Red Sea). I was also responsible to
British Ambassadors, Ministers, High Commissioners and
Governors of territories within the Middle East area.

My task consisted in knowing in as much detail as possible

the threats to the area as a whole and in ensuring that we had the means, the knowledge and the understanding to counter them. To that end it was my responsibility to pass to MI5 the information of which they needed to be informed, and to feed to local authorities the information of which they needed to be aware. Also to advise the individual territories on their security organisation and practices. In many of the territories we had our own SIME representatives to liaise with and advise the local authorities.

To keep in touch with local authorities and our own representatives it was necessary for me to travel widely and often. Seeing people on their own ground is much more effective than correspondence. I was able to leave my Headquarters in good hands because I had a marvellous deputy – David Stewart CBE.

The following pages give some account of my journeyings, and of the facilities available to travellers at that time fifty years ago, and some description of some of the places which I had to visit. The information comes largely from my letters to my wife which, unknown to me at the time, she kept.

The work consisted of identifying every subversive organisation which might be a threat to British security, and then of identifying every member of such organisations and recording their identities and details. Then of mounting the necessary measures to prevent them from being employed where they might be a threat to British security interests, normally by instituting and using effective vetting procedures. Also of designing and instructing effective protection against sabotage planned to damage premises or property of security importance. Furthermore, we had to know in detail the espionage threats and to ensure that adequate counter-espionage measures were in force and efficient.

As I surveyed the Middle East from my desk in General Headquarters, I wondered what the future would be. The component countries had had little experience of self-government. They had been for centuries, since the Middle Ages, part of the fluctuating Turkish or Ottoman Empire which dissolved after its defeat in the First World War. Its former territories, which were now my concern, therefore lacked experience of self-government, having from time to time, during the past six centuries, at best been semi-autonomous. Considerable instability seemed unavoidable, and there seemed a strong likelihood of military dictatorships emerging on the pattern of Turkey after the First World War. Britain still had her empire, although her hold on it had been much lessened by the Second World War, and a secure Middle East was one of the pillars of imperial strategy. Those of us who had some responsibility for trying to ensure stable conditions faced no shortage of work. There was a constant and major threat to the whole area. It was being flooded with subversion propaganda by Soviet Russia, and disaffected agents were being trained in Moscow. The Soviet was intent on destabilising the Middle East. I was heavily committed to keeping it stable.

The earliest of my letters to survive after I had taken up my appointment in Egypt is one from Fayid dated 8 September 1947:

> I was very sorry to leave Palestine, but I am nevertheless enjoying myself here. I have lots to do and it is interesting. Life of course isn't over-comfortable, but we are so busy that we haven't time to think about the grouses. These things are really relative. Fifty years ago people worried no end about the kind of starch used in their shirts. Nowadays we think ourselves lucky if we can buy a shirt at all and we have forgotten what starch looks like. The sort of food and comfort we have in messes now we would not have tolerated in camp before the war; but we have grown used to it.
>
> It has been fairly hot here with temperatures up to 106°, but it is nothing like India and it always cools down at night.

Fayid is in the desert, and we lived there in hutted accommodation. Our offices were Nissen huts; our living quarters for the most part rather superior huts. But there was much to be said for it. It was a good climate, dry, not too hot, and with a fresh breeze every afternoon off the sapphire blue expanse of the Great Bitter Lake. It was mostly gloriously sunny in winter and not cold. The rugged barren pink Suez mountains to the south gave added interest to the landscape. Besides the fishing boats on the lake – the elegant Egyptian feluccas – there was a constant, endlessly watchable, procession of shipping passing through it, as a part of the Suez Canal. Ships could only pass through the canal in one direction at a time, so they used to anchor in the lake as at a road block, waiting, as it were, to be given the green light.

There was a tremendous wool boom in Australia, and many rich Australians came home on ships via the Suez Canal (there were no passenger aircraft at that time) to enjoy a few weeks in England. A story went the rounds of one of them buying a Rolls-Royce which he took back to Australia. There one of his friends asked him how he was getting on with his new car.

'It's wonderful,' said the owner. 'The manufacturers have thought of everything. They've even put a glass screen between me and the back seat to stop the sheep from licking the back of my neck!'

Maxine had rented a house in the south of England, but my parents were very kindly ready to have her and the children to stay at any time at their home in Ireland, and for as long as she liked. They were elderly people living a quiet life, and it was good of them to be prepared to put up with all the noise and activity of two young children. But they had a large old Irish house with plenty of room outside as well as inside – extensive grounds with a river running through the place – and my father, in particular, was very fond of Maxine and greatly enjoyed having her company. My mother could not give him the really lively companionship that he particularly enjoyed. She was so deaf that it was hard to carry on a conversation with her, and she was no match for his quick and capacious mind.

There is another letter from Fayid, dated 15 December 1947. I had been back in London for talks with MI5, and my letter briefly describes passenger flying in those days before the days of jet, or turbo-prop, aircraft, or pressurised cabins, and when aircraft usually cruised at about 6,000-8,000 feet. Flying was more interesting then. We had a much better view of the ground. Indeed, we were not very high above it in hilly country. We sometimes even flew between hills, and we had to dodge round storms. There was no heating in aircraft, and no pressurised cabins. I don't know whether 13,000 feet was considered the safe limit without special oxygen arrangements – I flew several times at that height but never higher.

A letter dated Christmas Day 1947:

I went up to Jerusalem this day last week. I had a very nice flight in a small twin-engined aircraft with General MacMillan and we landed at the little airstrip in the hills a few miles from Jerusalem in a place named Kollundia.

I found them all in great form in Jerusalem, although the situation is as bad as ever – in some ways worse.

I dined one night in the General's mess and had a very pleasant evening among old friends – it was somewhere near two o'clock before I got to bed. I had lunch another day with the High Commissioner [General Sir Alan Cunningham] which I always enjoy. It is a beautiful house with a lovely garden and wonderful views over the Jordan valley and of the city of Jerusalem and the Mount of Olives. I was also bidden to a cocktail party by the Police at their mess and afterwards dined *à deux* with the Inspector General. He sent me back in his bullet-proof car as I was living the other side of the town. It is a city of the dead at night. There is not a soul in the streets except an odd police patrol – and not even a light in the windows.

I also had a number of other invitations so was kept pretty well entertained. I got through all my business successfully and flew back on Monday evening, but I shall probably have to go up to Jerusalem again in about a fortnight's time.

Things are very gay here. The Commander-in-Chief gave a great ball on Tuesday night. It was just like old times. I really thoroughly enjoyed it – we were not in bed until nearly 4 a.m. At about 6.30 in the evening, just before the dance, all the lights fused in Fayid and they did not get them going again until 9.15. The dance was billed for 9.30. Mrs McCall, the Admiral's wife, told me that she asked General Crocker [the Commander-in-Chief] what he thought when the lights went out. He replied, 'I was sitting in my bath at the time, and I burst into tears.'

Last night we had our Christmas dinner in the mess. It was really quite amusing to see a lot of elderly bachelors and grass-widowers rather solemnly doing Christmas *comme il faut* with some gravity – pulling crackers and adjusting their paper hats.

From Fayid, 11 January 1948:

Palestine is beginning to feel the withdrawal of Pax Britannica. There was sporadic shooting all day in Jerusalem, ending with quite a spirited shooting match right under the windows of the King David Hotel in the evening in which the Jews and Arabs must have fired a few hundred rounds at each other. It's as much as a Jew's life is worth to wander into an Arab area and vice versa. All the good Jewish shops in the main streets are closed. Many of them have had their windows smashed, and some are even burnt out. The future is quite unpredictable but, whatever it brings, Jerusalem is going to be the most difficult problem to solve. It is hard to see how UNO is going to come and turn it into an international zone. It has over 150,000 inhabitants, 90,000 of whom are Jews. The population of the immediately surrounding area, including Bethlehem, would probably make the Arab numbers up to about equal to the Jews. Jerusalem's water supply is very vulnerable, being piped in for many miles across the hills. Essential services, electric light, etc. are not much less so. The place is dependent for fuel on oil brought by rail or road from Haifa, and for food on communications running through areas which are entirely Arab. So how UN officials from a number of different countries, without an experienced Police Force, Army and Civil Administration, are going to keep Jerusalem supplied and functioning, and keep the Jews and Arabs from killing each other, is not at this moment quite clear; and UNO has just four months in which to get it clear before we give up our mandate.

I have lost my German batman. He has been repatriated on compassionate grounds to the Russian zone of Germany. He was a very nice man, so I hope he won't find himself in some Russian concentration camp. I am sorry to lose him. I now have another. Not, I think, so good.

I no longer recall what our policy was towards German prisoners of war, or how it came about that we still had unrepatriated prisoners as late as 1948, nearly three years after the end of the war with Germany. I suppose we were entitled to offer them jobs so long as they were with us. At all events, I had a very agreeable relationship with my German batman, and he not only seemed perfectly content to work for me but went out of his way to be helpful and to ease my personal life for me. I felt I had lost a friend when he went, and I was very concerned about what might face him when he got home. I felt it might be fatal to ask him to write to me.

From Fayid, 25 January 1948, to Maxine:

My parish has now been considerably enlarged to include all your uncle's kingdom (East Africa). [Maxine's uncle was Sir Philip Mitchell, KCMG, MC, Governor first of Uganda and then of Kenya.]However, I can take it. I shall have to make a trip down there soon and have a look round, but there is enough going on to tie me down here at the moment.

I have bought myself one of those awful ball bearing fountain pens [the 'biro' was then a new invention] so that I shall be able to write letters while I am on a trip. I never do manage to have a fountain pen in working order, and anyway they are no use when one is flying as all they do is spout ink all over your clothes.

[104]

I had an interesting trip to Jerusalem. I set off in a Proctor – a little single-engined aircraft – with Brigadier Dudley Hogg, a colleague here. I sat in front next to the driver, and Dudley sat in the back seat. It was a windy morning and we went along well with the wind behind us until we got to the Judean foothills when we got into low cloud. We were flying at 3,200 feet. I thought we were a bit low as Jerusalem is 3,600 with higher hills around. It was very windy and gusty and we got thrown about a bit flying rather low over the hills and valleys. Eventually the cloud, which was down almost to ground level, got pretty thick so the pilot decided to clear out. I reckoned we were then about Hebron.

We circled to the east before turning out for the plain to the west. I presumed that the best etiquette was not to talk to the man at the wheel, though I had been thinking for some time of telling him to go a bit higher as I was not sure whether he really knew the country. When he turned further into the hills to circle I suggested to him that he should go up a bit as I knew there was something about 4,000 feet near Hebron. We got out over the plain and I saw a village I knew so was able to tell him where we were. We then went up north and landed at Ein Shemer airfield. It was raining, squally and with a very strong wind. At Ein Shemer they told us it was OK at Kollundia, the little airfield in the hills near Jerusalem. I didn't see how it could be as the clouds were down on top of the hills.

Anyway we set off again as I still felt one should leave it to the man at the wheel. We flew south through a heavy rainstorm preparatory to turning into the hills when we got level with Jerusalem. He was a very good pilot, covered with decorations, but I felt that perhaps he had the idea that, having two VIP passengers, he must get them to their destination at all costs. So, as I know what the weather is like in those hills in those conditions, and I considered that to try to get into Kollundia would be unnecessarily foolish, I told him to land at Lydda (in the plain) – which he did, and we then got a car down from Jerusalem and went up by road.

The same chap was to fly up and fetch us two days later. However, the RAF said the weather was too bad for flying and wouldn't send a plane. It struck me as a good deal better than the day we left although the wind was still very high, so I feared I had made an aeronautical blot by 'talking to the man at the wheel' and that the RAF had been piqued. However, I got a chance to talk to the pilot's boss later and sounded him on the question. He said I was quite right, and that one is always right to direct a pilot if you think there is any danger of which he may be unaware – so relations with the RAF are still OK, which is as well as I depend a lot on them.

As a matter of fact I enjoyed the trip. It's always interesting to watch an expert doing his business when he is up against something which tests him a bit. This chap made beautiful landings despite the very high wind, and his boss said that it is not a good thing flying light aircraft in a high wind, which was genuinely the reason why they have all been grounded during the gales we have had here for the last few days.

We had to come down by train from Lydda. A slow, wobbly and very dusty journey.

There was a hell of a battle going on in Jerusalem when we got there between the Jews and Arabs. At least they fired off an enormous amount of ammunition. One of my pals up there, Tom Page, a Gunner lieutenant-colonel, told me that he watched the whole battle from the King David – a couple of hundred yards from where it was taking place – and he thought the Arabs had taken an awful pasting and that they would not want a lot of that sort of thing if they got the same medicine from every Jewish position they attacked. On the other hand I had a talk with a newspaper man who was with the Jews and he said it was exceedingly unpleasant and he reckoned they were about finished when the battle stopped. British troops did not intervene in these encounters.

I stayed this time with the GOC, General MacMillan, in Jerusalem. He has a most beautiful house. I have often been there but had never slept in it before. It was built by a Jewish South African diamond-king and is the last word in everything modern. My bedroom was a most cunning affair of cupboards, hot and cold water, central heating, ventilation, etc., and most economical of space. The house is just a bit too angular to be friendly, and too exact to be quite human. But there's no doubt that modern houses are the thing to live in, and double glass windows are a wonderful idea for keeping you either warm or cool.

I came in for a cocktail party at Government House where I met a lot of old friends. It was, as usual, a very good show and I enjoyed it. I managed to get the High Commissioner, General Sir Alan Cunningham, away to his study for a bit during the party and had a useful chat with him. He is such a very nice man. I'm sure he'll be sorry to leave his house with its wonderful inspiring views, but it will be some relief to take that load of responsibility off his back.

I will probably go to Jerusalem once more before we finally evacuate, if I can make it. It is sad now to see everything being dismantled in southern Palestine. Camps and barracks which are left standing are just being looted.

Each time that I have been in Jerusalem recently, I have come in for a battle. The security situation has much deteriorated, with some consequent economic dislocation, but somehow life goes on and many people go normally about their affairs. Quite a lot of the shooting that goes on is pure nerves. For instance, there was a good lot of shooting going on all day when I was last there but it died down when it got dark. However, in the part of the town where I was staying, just as we were going to bed someone started up a motor bike which backfired a few times, whereupon shooting started again all over the place. Arabs and Jews have been murdering each other pretty freely and a war to the death is likely to start on the day we surrender the mandate. That is more or less the declared intention of both sides.

I hope to get up to Jerusalem once more before we finally evacuate it. I would like to get up sometime in April when the country looks at its best and all the flowers are in bloom.

I had to go to Jerusalem frequently to take part in the day-to-day planning to evacuate Palestine safely.

I accidentally spent an interesting day recently sightseeing in Cairo. I went up strictly on business to see someone who was passing through to the Far East by air. His plane was due to reach Cairo in the evening and to leave again early the next morning. The plane, a Constellation, came in on time after doing the journey from England in eight and a half hours. However, it was delayed the next day with some engine trouble, so I took it upon me to show my chap and a couple of other passengers a bit of Cairo. Incidentally the Constellation, which was destined for Australia, only lands four times between England and Australia – at Cairo, Karachi, Calcutta and Singapore.

I got hold of an archaeologist friend to act as guide. We first went to the museum and looked at the Tutankhamen treasures. As Emery, the archaeologist [Professor Bryan Emery, who later had the chair of Egyptology at London University], had actually worked on the tomb, there was nothing about it that he did not know and it was an interesting experience having him to explain it all. I never tire of Tutankhamen. Some of the things which came out of the tomb must be among the most beautiful in the world.

Then, after a quick look at a cross-section of the rest of the museum, we went out to have a look at the Pyramids. I had not visited them since I got off a boat at Suez in 1932, dashed to Cairo for the day, and joined the boat again at Port Said. It is their enormous mass which is so impressive. They are man-made mountains constructed of huge blocks of stone. They must have been very beautiful as they were encased in a very hard polished white limestone. There are only a few pieces of it left now. It was not time which removed the outer casing, but the Arabs who used the Pyramids as quarries when they were building Cairo in the thirteenth century! Similar vandalism was going on in Persia when I was there, where the Persians were breaking up the beautiful fallen columns of Darius's palaces at Persepolis to make road metal.

From Fayid, 28 February 1948:

I have fixed my trip to East Africa for 10 March. I go to Asmara in Eritrea first and then to Aden; then Hargeisha in what had been British Somaliland, then Mogadishu in what had been Italian Somaliland, both now Somalia; then Nairobi, then Khartoum and then back here about the beginning of April.

In all these places I had to discuss the possible threats to their security, and to advise the administrators on the protective measures they should take. I also had to study the local situations and conditions for my own understanding.

9
East African Journey

From Hargeisa, British Somaliland, 17 March 1948, to Maxine:

> I am now in British Somaliland. I got here yesterday morning and cannot get on to Mogadishu until Sunday 21 March, which gives me a good deal more time than I want. I am adding some notes. On the whole I am taking things pretty easily because, owing to limited transport, I have to spend more time than I need in each place and so I am enjoying having something of a laze.
>
> The Governor of British Somaliland, Fisher – your father would remember – was in the F & P [Indian Foreign and Political Service] and was Resident at Gwalior one time when your Pa went down there.
>
> It is very much out of the world here. The local problems loom large and are in themselves large, but there are no newspapers and I only hear snatches of world news from anyone who happens to have listened to the wireless.

Notes written on my journey from Egypt to British Somaliland, and enclosed with my above letter:

Note 1, Aden: I left Fayid by car after lunch on 11 March for Cairo where I had to spend the night as we were due to make an early start the next morning.

I was hauled out of bed at 2.30 a.m. next day, but we were a bit late starting and did not take off until nearly 5.30 a.m. Our aircraft was a BOAC [British Overseas Airways Corporation] Dakota. It was a freight machine and so not particularly comfortable, though the seats were good.

Our first stop was Luxor, which we reached after a couple of hours' flying. Luxor is little more than a village in the green strip of the Nile valley. It looked very pretty and fresh in the early morning light, and the hills surrounding it were lovely pale pink and mauve colours.

We did not, of course, have any time for sightseeing, and I failed to spot the Valley of the Kings; but the huge temples etc., which I think date from about 1300 BC and are out in the middle of the valley, were clearly visible from the air as we came in to land.

We only stopped in Luxor long enough to refuel and have a cup of tea, and then took off again for the port of Jedda on the Saudi Arabian coast of the Red Sea.

We flew first over the extraordinary desert of Upper Egypt. It is an ochre brown colour streaked here and there with red and golden sands, and out of it jut precipitous Dantesque pillars of black rock rising in places to perhaps seven or eight thousand feet.

Looking at that desert bathed in the red light of the early morning sun you have the eerie feeling that you are thrown back millions of years to the dawn of time, to the very same scene the first prehistoric monster looked on as he dragged his sluggish way from the deep and surveyed the world. Day after day, year after year, century upon century for millions of years, the sun rises and sets upon it. At night it cools and the moon casts weird shadows amongst the black rock mountains, but all is dead and there the whole scene stands generation after generation, never changing except for the creeping of the sand when the wind stirs, and the slow crumbling of the rocks.

We flew out across the Red Sea and landed at Jedda. The harbour consists of nothing but a few reefs and shoals. There is a 'modern' town standing on the bare desert, and alongside it the ancient town which is just mud huts.

Jedda is the chief port of Saudi Arabia and best known as the place of entry for pilgrims to the holy cities. The airfield is just the flat clay desert, and the airport little more than a caravanserai with no comforts for passengers. Sitting about in it were a lot of Arabs who, I suppose, have little to do except sit about; and standing in the sand were numbers of beautiful high-powered American cars. Every now and again an Arab would get up and get into one of the cars and drive off in a cloud of dust.

There was a door in the caravanserai labelled 'Jedda Airport Buffet'. It was full of smoke, and dark, with strange smells, a contrast to BOAC air hostesses in 'New Look' clothes dispensing comforts to passengers on the European services. ['New Look' was the ladies' fashion of the time.]

From Jedda we flew south and crossed the Red Sea again and landed on the east shore at Port Sudan. A glance from the air showed it to be unmistakably British: everything laid out neatly, and nice little red-roofed bungalows each standing in its own garden. We refuelled once more and set off at about 1.30 p.m. We climbed to 10,000 feet and flew south over the Eritrean mountains and landed at the capital of Eritrea, Asmara, which is on a plateau about 8,000 feet up, and where we were to night-stop. [Eritrea had been a part of Italian colonial territory. After the Second World War it was administered by Britain and in 1962 it became a province of Ethiopia.]

I have an officer there, who met me at the airport and he and his wife took me back to tea. I then inspected the office and did such work as I had to do until dinner time. The security problems in Eritrea are not yet acute.

Asmara, built by the Italians, is a lovely little town with a truly wonderful climate. It has beautiful gardens and flowering trees and shrubs. All the English flowers grow in great profusion, and to prize-winning dimensions, without much attention. I had a good night's sleep in the clean and comfortable modern Italian hotel there, and we were off again for Aden at 8.30 next morning.

We flew straight eastwards off the red-brown plateau,

over green hills and across the plain towards the coast. The plain was covered in a blanket of low cloud, and it must have been very hot and steamy below. When we reached the coast the cloud cleared and we headed out to sea for the island of Kamaran near the Arabian coast.

Although we had had fine weather all the way, the atmosphere was hazy and visibility not very good all along the Red Sea, but everything had a mother-of-pearl look, and the many islands and shoals in the southern part of the Red Sea were very pretty in the early morning light.

After a couple of hours' flying, we landed at Kamaran Island and were swept back to the British Empire of half a century ago. It is just a flat desert island, with little or nothing growing on it, and a few square miles in extent. We were greeted warmly by the Governor, a Major Thompson, whose old Ford car flying a large Union Jack stood outside the hutment which serves as the airport. Three flagpoles stood up from the roof of the hut, each carrying a Union Jack, and between the flagpoles were strung on two lines the flags of other nations with a good many more Union Jacks. The hutment itself was plastered with photos of the Royal Family and British leaders. A lady on the plane told me that there was even a photo in the ladies' lavatory of the Queen, and two of Princess Elizabeth.

Major Thompson was also an old-world type with the leisure to be affable, hospitable and self-assured, and with a bristling moustache. As we boarded the plane to take off, he shook hands with each passenger, raised his hat and bid us goodbye. He had no problems of concern to me.

From Kamaran we flew down the Arabian coast and soon ran into bad weather; a high wind from the south east; some cloud, and quantities of dust up to six or seven thousand feet. Over the island of Perim, which is at the entrance to the Red Sea, we turned eastwards and flew along the coast to Aden.

Long years ago when a P&O liner, returning to England from India, was heading for the Red Sea on a dark night, the first class passengers gave a party to which they invited the ship's officers. They came, leaving the youngest officer on the bridge to keep the watch, and with instructions to steer for Perim Island – which he did with such accuracy that he hit it. Thereafter P&O officers were debarred from attending passengers' parties.

It is very much hotter here in Aden than in Egypt. Though the temperature indoors is only in the low eighties, it is damp. There is no need for a blanket at night.

I had an office there; and both the Aden Colony and the Protectorate were facing considerable security problems which came to a head after I had left the Middle East. One of our officers' wives was later killed in a terrorist outrage.

Note 2, Hargeisa: I left Aden by BOAC Dakota on the morning of 16 March early. It was a fully-furnished and comfortable machine. It was cloudy, and we went up through the cloud and then flew above it at 6,000 feet. We were above the cloud the whole way until we came within a few miles of Hargeisa [the capital of what was then British Somaliland].

In British Somaliland we are in what is known as the Horn of Africa – that part of Africa which juts out eastwards into the Indian Ocean south of the Red Sea. Most of the territories there have changed hands up to three times in the past sixty years. It is therefore difficult to describe.

Hargeisa is about 4,500 feet above sea level; a little place with an entirely Somali population except for the British officials connected with the administration. The country round is an undulating, brown, arid plateau, covered with scrub and thorn trees. It is not unlike parts of northern India.

It is a good bit cooler and drier than Aden and everyone here says it is an excellent climate. Personally I find it at first very enervating and relaxing, but I have frequently encountered that feeling in places which are fairly high up and at the same time warm. There are no fans here so it apparently does not get very hot.

I was met at the airport by a young officer who took me to the little NAAFI club where I spent the night. Both the Governor and the local OC Troops had kindly wished to accommodate me but were full up last night as the General Officer Commanding, East African Command, the AOC [Air Officer Commanding] Aden and the AOC East Africa were here on tour with some of their staff. Indeed the OC Troops told me he spent last night sleeping on a rug on his drawing room floor! However, 'the captains and the kings' departed by air this morning and Mr Fisher, the Governor, took me in and I am now among the fleshpots.

I gather there are lots of game birds – bustard, francolin, sand grouse, guinea fowl, etc. Also quantities of big game – mostly antelope of many species, leopard, and a great many lions. There are no rhinos, and there is only one elephant left in British Somaliland.

I was invited to a cocktail party at the HQ Officers' Mess last night which was given in honour of the big shots – useful to me as I met a good many people. Afterwards one of the officers, a Major Drysdale, asked me back to his house where he had arranged a cold supper for some of his friends. It was like old days and I enjoyed it. The talk was of shooting and ballistics, horses, dogs, etc., plus local problems and 'shop'.

Drysdale had a couple of cheetah cubs in his house a few weeks old. They were very tame but rather ugly with large heads and thick shaggy coats and a grey woolly ruff down their backs. A cheetah is somewhere between a dog and a cat but it is neither. Perhaps it should be described as a doglike cat or a pussdog. They grow into the most beautiful animals and become completely tame. They do not turn treacherous like so many wild animals when they grow up and find their strength. They become just like dogs and you can have them round the house like a dog.

The Somalis are slim dark people with thick fuzzy hair, and akin to the Abyssinians; but unlike the Abyssinians, who are Christians, they are Muslims. They live for the most part a nomadic tribal life following the rains and the grazings.

The country has been left politically and socially very unsettled by the war, and there are potentialities for trouble. I discussed these fully with the local administration, and advised on measures to counter them.

From Hargeisa, British Somaliland, 20 March 1948 (Note 3):

I am due to move on tomorrow to Mogadishu in Somalia. [It was formerly Italian Somaliland, but after the Second World War was administered by Britain. In 1960 British Somaliland and Somalia continued as the independent state of Somalia.] Having got used to the climate here and got over the lethargy which I felt for the first day or two, I have found it very pleasant. The Fishers have been most kind and hospitable and I have lived in great comfort.

The birds are quite fascinating. Two weaver birds, one canary-coloured, and the other grey and white, and black on top, with a crimson splash under his tail, seem fairly common. There are also little short-tailed parrots. I have not had a good look at them but they are a flash of metallic green with a scarlet breast as they fly past. There is a lovely bee-eater which is neither the green bee-eater nor the blue-tailed bee-eater. Green, gold, copper and black are his colours. I have seen partridge and a francolin. There is a fine crested magpie, many doves, and also Cape of Good Hope rock pigeons – the latter, I believe, imported. There is also a drongo called the Abyssinian crow. And numerous other birds I have never seen before, even though the same species may exist elsewhere – for instance a sunbird not unlike the Indian purple sunbird. But the gayest chap of all is a starling; there are flocks of them. He has a bright green throat and upper breast, and a red tummy and undertail. The green and red are separated by a thin line of pure white which goes right round his thorax. The whole of his back and wings are a deep shiny royal blue. I can't see one at the moment, but I have an impression of a red bill and red legs.

The population of this country, which is some 350 miles long by 150 deep at its broadest, is estimated to be about 700,000. No census has ever been attempted. Virtually their only occupation is the breeding of camels, cattle, sheep and goats. Their income is derived from the sale of hides and skins, of which two to three millions are exported annually, and of some meat on the hoof sent principally to Aden. They grow very little grain, fruit or vegetables, and their food consists primarily of milk, a little imported grain and some meat. One would think that the export of so many hides might denote a fair consumption of meat but, as most of the leather consists of goat and sheep skins, and the animals are small, if you allow about 25-30 lb of meat at the outside per beast, a simple sum shows that the meat from the maximum number of skins exported would amount to 1 lb per day per head of the population for less than one third of the year. That would be a generous ration at home, but here there is virtually no other food. However, I understand that the position is nothing like as favourable as even these figures might suggest as most of the animals whose hides and skins are exported die of disease, starvation, lack of water, etc., and are not killed for meat. By the way, I understand that a *hide* is a large animal, camel or cattle, and a *skin* is a small one, sheep or goats.

The people, therefore, are extremely poor and under-nourished. There seem to be possibilities of developing the natural food resources in two ways. First by developing fisheries. There is apparently a vast untapped wealth of fish in this part of the Indian Ocean. Secondly by drying and storing milk in the rainy season.

I understand that it might also be possible to get more attractive prices for skins if a regular supply of well-tanned material could be assured to manufacturers of high-grade luxury leather articles. The reason is that the sheep in this and some other parts of Africa have hair instead of wool. Wool derives from a concentrated curling stem of wool fibres which are already curling before they leave the skin. The result is somewhat coarse and spongy leather. Hair gives a much finer grained leather suitable for such things as ladies' gloves.

There is also a possibility of the development of another smaller but potentially valuable industry as a by-product of both skin and fish, namely sharkskin. I am told that on any afternoon you can catch half a dozen sharks off the Somaliland coast with a hook and handline within thirty yards of the shore. It is believed that sharks exist in these waters in huge numbers and that an aim to export 250,000 skins a year might even prove to be conservative. Well, hides and skins etc. aren't my business and these are just a few crumbs of information I have come by and which I find quite interesting.

However, the trouble with the development of a country of this sort is that it does not perhaps tend to improve the welfare of the wretched people. Their standard of living is so low that you would have to increase the wealth of the individual perhaps tenfold before he would really reach a state where he would himself see the point of aiming at a better way of life. So that all that happens as you increase the wealth is that the population also increases and the individual standard of living remains much the same. Ecclesiastes, chapter 5, verse 11: 'When goods increase, they are increased that eat them.'

When India gained her independence in 1947, the then truncated India had a population of 250 million. The Indian peasantry had preserved their soil structure for at least 6,000 years by careful conservation. They could not return much humus to the soil because they had to burn dung because there was nothing else to burn. They ploughed very shallow with a wooden ox plough. They only broke the surface of the soil, left it lumpy and did not reduce it to a fine tilth, and they used a low-yielding seed. The result was a subsistence level of living which was tolerable and durable

For the past fifty years the Indian peasantry have ploughed and harrowed with tractors. They have ploughed deep and reduced the soil to a fine tilth. They have then used artificial fertilisers and a high-yielding seed, and as a result have harvested four or five times the old crop, and as a result of that the population has increased at the same rate and now is 900 million, but the standard of living remains the same subsistence level of the old-day Indian peasant. The result in 100 years' time may, I fear, be a dust bowl with devastating famines. It may come to be one of the world's great disasters.

From Mogadishu, Somalia, 21 March 1948:

I arrived here at 11.20 a.m. today after four hours' flight from Hargeisa. The aircraft, belonging to a company operating locally between Aden and Nairobi, was a very old Anson. However, although it looked a most uncertain affair, and the engines sounded none too sweet, it seemed to go all right. I gather forced landings are not uncommon, but they have so far avoided a serious accident.

Having only been here an hour, I have neither met my host, Brigadier Smith, the Chief Administrator of Somalia, nor seen anything of the place. The climate at the moment is not as bad as I thought it might be. It is hottish and stickyish, but doesn't compare with the rains in India.

There is a small Italian population here, and a number of modern buildings and a few Fascist frills reflecting the glory that was Rome. The town is built on the sea front and all around is the usual scrub desert. There is a fairly strong wind blowing and the sea looks most invitingly clean and fresh.

Brigadier Smith has the Duke of Aosta's residence. It is not exactly palatial as it only has one bedroom. I am sleeping in the guest house nearby.

In the air, 24 March 1948:

I have been very busy ever since I arrived in Mogadishu and got no time for letter-writing. However, I knew I would have some hours in the air during which I could write. This ball bearing pen is a horrible thing, but it certainly is exceedingly useful.

I did little in Mogadishu except work. Indeed, until just before sundown yesterday evening I spent the whole time either interviewing people or writing notes.

The Horn of Africa was ripe for security problems, particularly political subversion from Ethiopia and armed conflict between the various factions. I explained this in detail, and individually addressed each of the people who would be likely to be personally involved. From these interviews I also greatly increased my own knowledge and understanding of the local conditions.

Note 4, in the air between Mogadishu and Nairobi, 24 March 1948:

Of twenty towns in Somalia with a population of more than a 1,000, only four have 10,000, and only one of those, Mogadishu, has more than 10,000. It has a population of 65,000. Of these some 3,000 are Italians and the remainder Somalis, except for a few Indian and Arab traders, and British officials. There are a lot of good Italian buildings in it, including a fine RC cathedral, and from the harbour it is a pretty town. The harbour itself is shallow and even small ships have to lie outside. There is a wonderful bathing beach – beautiful white sand and clear water and protected from sharks by a reef about a mile out to sea.

On the whole the climate is not bad though it must become a little monotonous. Being almost on the equator, the seasons are seasons of rain and not of the sun. The temperature seldom goes above 90°F day or night, and seldom falls below 70°F. It is humid, but a good fresh breeze blows for all except a couple of months of the year.

I have now acquired some history of the Somalis. Their

origin is obscure but the following general idea seems more acceptable than any other. We have to start at the beginning.

Anthropologically, the Eurasian and African peoples can be divided into three main races: the Caucasoid in the north (Europe, North Africa and the Middle East); the Negroes south of the equator; and, in between, the Negroid, where the other two have intermingled.

Traditionally, the northern Caucasoid race is divided into three main groups deriving from the three sons of Noah, Shem, Ham and Japheth. From Shem (or Sem) spring the Semites including the Jews and the pure Arabs. From Ham spring the Hamites or Hemitic group. From Japheth spring the Aryans.

We are now concerned only with the Hamitic group. Ham had four sons one of whom was Cush, and from him derived a people known as the Kushites (spelt with either a 'C' or a 'K') who became settled south of Babylon at the head of the Persian Gulf.

The Egyptians derived from another of Ham's sons; the Berbers of North Africa from a third; and the Phoenicians, who are now scattered, were descended from the fourth.

Ancient Egyptian inscriptions between the twenty-second and the seventeenth centuries BC record the migration to the Nile valley, presumably by way of the Indian Ocean and the Red Sea, of Kushite immigrants from the Persian Gulf area, and the establishment of a kingdom of Kush probably between the third and sixth cataracts on the Nile.

In about 2700 BC the Egyptians built a road 150 miles long from the Red Sea to a place on the Nile just north of Luxor named Coptos. (Coptos is the Greek name for Egypt.) Possibly the Kushites used this road to reach the Nile. Its purpose was to facilitate the luxury trade in gold, ivory, slaves, incense, myrrh, etc. from the south through the Red Sea. It is from Coptos that the name of the Coptic Christian religion of the Abyssinians derives.

It then appears that these Hamitic Kushites, who settled

in the Nile valley, and possibly along the western shore of the Red Sea, gradually pushed (and possibly were pushed) southwards into the rich uplands of Eritrea and Abyssinia and fanned out southwards along the coasts of Eritrea and the Somalilands and as far as Kenya. Their history must, of course, have been influenced by the history of Egypt; and the influences in the area of the Egyptians, Persians, Greeks, Romans, etc., and also by Arab developments.

Along the coastal areas the Kushites have mixed with the Semitic Arabs, and in the southern area they have mixed with the Negroes to form Negroid stock in places, but it is possible that in the central part of the area they now inhabit, which is mainly the highlands of Abyssinia, the stock is still pure Hamitic.

An early landmark in their history is about the year 1000 BC. Their kingdom was at that time known as the Kingdom of Axum (alternatively Aksum) and the Queen of Sheba was on the throne. With the help of the Phoenicians, Solomon, king of the Jews, being a man of energy and vision, started to push his trade into the Arabian and African coasts about the southern Red Sea area. This was definitely poaching on the rich preserves of the Queen of Sheba, so she set off on a diplomatic mission to Jerusalem. Her diplomatic entente with Solomon was sealed and ratified by the somewhat unusual method of the birth of a son who was named Menelek-ibu-Hakim, and it is from him that the late royal family of Abyssinia claims descent. (Sheba was an ancient kingdom incorporating parts of southern Arabia.)

In the fourth century AD, under the influence of the Roman Emperor Constantine, the kingdom of Axum adopted Christianity.

The year 632, a fateful year for much of the world, is the next date of importance. The Prophet Mohammed died, and the impact of the faith he had founded began to shake great areas of Europe, Asia and Africa. Before long Muslim missionaries, bringing Islamic zeal, and refugees from Arabia began to arrive on the coast of the Horn of Africa. It so happened that almost coincidental with this Islamic development, the Kushite kingdom of Axum disintegrated with the flight of the royal family in AD 650. There was therefore fertile ground for the Islamic missionaries. Islam spread rapidly along the coastal area and inland, except in the highlands where Christianity retained its hold. It was thus that this people became divided into the two main divisions which exist today, the Mohammedan Somalis in the areas near the coast, the Christian Abyssinians inland

The origin of the word Somali is obscure but it is certain that it derives from Islamic times.

There has been much unrest in the Horn of Africa since the coming of Islam in the seventh century AD, mostly in the form of struggles between the Christian Abyssinians and the Muslim Somalis.

Somewhere about AD 1000 the Imam of Muscat, at the mouth of the Persian Gulf, extended his influence down the coast of Arabia, into the Red Sea and along the East African coast. For the next 500 years he and his descendants, and those of his governors, maintained, with fluctuating fortune, their influence along the coast. In 1499 Vasco da Gama sailed round the Cape and, before going on to India, anchored at Mogadishu. In the next 150 years, the Portuguese, although their fortunes also fluctuated, were paramount along the East African coast. Thereafter their influence began to decline and, from 1660 onwards, that of the Imams of Muscat once more began to increase. The Imam of Muscat moved his residence to Zanzibar, and the present Sultan of Zanzibar is his descendant.

From the time when Portuguese influence in the Indian Ocean declined, there took place in India the struggle for power between the British and French. Neither wished to antagonise the Imam of Muscat whose strategic position and personal influence were both important, so it was in the interests of both to support him. Consequently he remained in some immunity, ruling somewhat loosely over the east coast of Africa from the south of the Red Sea to Mozambique until the end of the Napoleonic wars when Britain formally recognised his sovereignty in this area.

From the middle of the nineteenth century dates the carving up of Africa by the European powers into spheres of influence. After considerable diplomatic chicanery and double-dealing Tanganyika went to the Germans (to be mandated to Britain after the First World War by the League of Nations). Kenya went to the British. The whole of Somalia, Abyssinia and Eritrea were agreed to be Italian spheres of interest, and British and French interests were recognised in British and French Somaliland.

The Italians, however, soon found themselves in trouble. The Abyssinians resented their interference and resisted it, and then in 1889 there came to the throne of Abyssinia a remarkable man named Menelek II. He greatly increased his kingdom not only by subduing other Christian Abyssinian chieftains but also at the expense of the Somalis and the Italians. Finally, in 1896, he completely defeated the Italian forces at the Battle of Adowa in northern Abyssinia. Of a force of 8,000 Italian and 6,000 native troops, 5,000 Italians were left dead on the field. Menelek did not, however, follow up his victory and subsequently a treaty was negotiated with Italy whereby she retained Eritrea and Italian Somaliland, and Menelek retained Abyssinia.

In 1935/6 the Italians, as part of Mussolini's empire-building, captured the whole of Abyssinia. But after Italy's declaration of war on us in 1940, we cut off 300,000 of her best troops in this African area.

This put an end to Italian colonial claims in this area. Italian Somaliland was lost to the Italians and joined to British Somaliland to become the Somalia of today

The ancient history of this area has not yet fully run its

course. The ancient peoples from the north are still exerting pressure southwards on the northern borders of Kenya.

From Nairobi, Kenya, Easter Sunday, 28 March 1948, to Maxine:

Your uncle and aunt [Sir Philip Mitchell, the Governor of Kenya, and his wife] asked me to stay, so I am installed in comfort and magnificence in Government House. They have both been very kind. They certainly are wonderful hosts. Your aunt runs the place with impressive efficiency.

I need hardly say that we have the peerage here, Lord and Lady De La Warr – 'Bucky' because he used to be Lord Buckhurst. His wife is a quite charming person with a delightful sense of humour.

We have also had the Negley Farsons [well-known American author who wrote on Africa] staying here. I would say she had the brains in that outfit.

There has also been a very high-powered lady staying, Dame Margery Perham, an Oxford don. She disposes of cabinet ministers and all the great ones by their christian names.

If you stayed in this house long enough, all the great in the land would have passed you in procession. But what I like about it is that I feel that the procession would not be dull. There would be both the great clerics and the great blackguards, as well as the rich and the poor and the halt and the maimed and the blind. There is no doubt that your uncle is a very big-hearted man, and he grows in stature on his own ground.

The rains have not started yet so the place is rather brown, but nevertheless I think it is quite lovely; all the flowering trees and shrubs are beautiful.

Today we went to church in the Cathedral. It was an extremely nice service with all the best hymns. The Cathedral was packed, with people even sitting on the altar steps.

On Good Friday afternoon, Lady De La Warr, Margery Perham and I went for a drive through the Game Reserve. We drove out to the Ngong hills and had a picnic tea there, and looked out for miles over the plains. It is certainly a curious country, but I can't help the feeling that it is not our world. It seems to have little connection with the world of men. Its history is not the history of the human race. The inhabitants are incidental. It is essentially primeval. Its last dynasty was the dinosaurs, whose successors are the elephant, the rhino and the hippo.

In the Game Reserve we saw zebra, impala, wildebeest, hartebeest, baboons, hyena, Thompson's gazelle, giraffe and the greater bustard. We saw no lion. I thought the Thompson's gazelle a most beautiful creature; I wish they had given him a more attractive name. I loved the giraffes. I had always thought them ungainly creatures, but in fact they are beautifully balanced and most graceful when they move, be it at a walk or a canter. They looked so fit and well, and there is something stimulating in the great power of their huge shoulders.

While I was in Nairobi I had talks with the heads of the police and the military and I had a long talk with Sir Philip Mitchell. Subversion was emanating from Moscow all over the Middle East and the colonial world, and the lower strata in Kenya were well enough educated to absorb it, and I urged Sir Philip to add a special branch to his police force with which my organisation would liaise closely. But he would not do it. He said Kenya had a limited budget and he felt that he must put all he could spare into education, and he said that he was quite satisfied that the police and the missionaries would know and would tell him if anything was going wrong. I said that the sort of dangerous activity about which I was speaking would be designed to avoid that sort of surveillance.

Later, he came home to retire. He had been promised a

peerage, because he was judged to be the finest Colonial administrator since Lugard. But, no sooner was he home than the serious Mau Mau rebellion broke out. There was by then a special branch in the police force, but it was too late, and Sir Philip did not get his peerage.

IO

Egyptian Interlude

From Fayid, Egypt, 8 April 1948, to Maxine:

I arrived back here to find my room had been burgled. My new black suit, my new overcoat and, alas! my old tweed suit, and some oddments gone. No hope of getting anything back though I might get some insurance money on the new things at any rate. There is an enormous amount of thieving here.

I may be wanted to make an inquiry into the conduct of our representative in Malta, which is not in my area of responsibility. I am not keen to take on something else as I have enough to keep me occupied.

However, I said I would do the job if they really can't produce anyone else. But this is just to let you know that I might be turning up sometime, because I may have to go home to report. I should think it will be within the next month, if it comes off. It's a bit awkward having no clothes now!

I am still pretty busy, but we are beginning to reap the fruits of sound policy, and the good chaps we got in are taking on more and more of the work as they get experienced. In some ways it creates more work as they do more, but a great deal now gets done with hardly a reference to me which formerly I would have had to do myself if I wanted to be sure it was done properly.

From Fayid, 25 April 1948:

I am glad the parcel turned up from Aden. There should be another little parcel turning up containing a cyclamen and more, but different, irises. They are from Palestine. The last

Maxine, 1940

The author and Maxine leaving the church after their wedding

A Kulu shepherd

Yezd, Persia. Author's sketch

A Persian highway

Persian tribeswomen   Tomb of Darius, Naksha-i-Rustum

An old Persian shepherd

The deserted mud-brick city of Bam

Four German parachutists being handed over to the author by a Persian tribe

Persepolis

Capture of Emperor Valerian by the Persians, Naksha-i-Rustum

Gateway to the old British Consulate, Shiraz

Author's friend Aga-i-Rouine, an addict, smoking opium

The author and Maxine, Delhi, 1945

time I was up there one of the girls, who was due to come down here, told me she was collecting some wild plants and I told her I was sure you would like cyclamen, irises and tulips if she could get them. She failed over the tulips, as I did last year. The trouble is that the bulb is very deep and really impossible to reach with a knife, which is the only tool one is likely to have in one's pocket.

From Fayid, 2 May 1948:

Your New Look efforts must at least be giving you plenty of scope for your ingenuity.

I would love to be home now to see all the flowers and blossom. There is no doubt that the wild flowers of the UK beat anything else. In Palestine or Persia one admires them in contrast to the desert, but they would pass unnoticed at home.

I am glad to hear that George is pleased with the idea of 'father coming' and says a little prayer for the poor chap – he needs it. I am sure he will remember me when he sees me, particularly if I have a ball to bounce for him.

I rather tend to agree with your father about stamps. I collected them in a very desultory way for a bit, but then I was not at all interested in many of the things which do interest boys. My greatest indoor pleasures were playing marbles and chess and reading historical novels. I had no interest in county cricket, league football, motor cars, railway engines and so forth. I had a passion for everything geographical (no doubt inherited from my mother) but that did not engender any interest in stamps, though I loved the ones with animals and landscapes on them. Portraits of a cut-throat President of some banana republic, however valuable, left me cold. My interest in birds' eggs and butterflies was also pretty desultory and, I think, rested entirely on colour and the mysteries accompanying rarity. The normal boy's (and indeed the normal man's) mind is not sufficiently meticulous and intensive for serious philately. I think I had a latent interest in drawing which, however, never ran into any encouraging force. I would have had wonderful opportunities for it as a boy which I think I missed simply because I thought that only very clever people could do it, and it was very evident to me that I didn't come into that category.

That's all about myself, but it seems as well, when considering children, to try to look back at one's own earlier life – which is a term that I prefer to childhood. I can't help a feeling that we tend to look upon children as different from ourselves but, looking back, I know that I was essentially the same, and in many ways as 'grown up', when I was eight years old as I am now. A child has many interests which we lose later in life but, in the child's own time, they are just as important as some of ours. The child also lacks, of course, much experience which enables us to adjust the details of our outlook – and which perhaps often tend to confuse the intuitive wisdom which we have when we are younger. On the whole, I am quite convinced that the more one treats children as grown ups the better.

I had a pleasant afternoon yesterday. One of my messmates asked me to go canoeing. His craft is a not very good two-seater into which I had to wedge my behind so tightly that I almost wondered how I would unstick myself if we capsized. There was not, however, much chance of that as it was a blazing hot, flat calm afternoon. I used to be an expert canoeist – acquired in the days of my youth. It was lovely out on the lake and I thoroughly enjoyed it.

From Fayid, 17 May 1948:

I supped with the Hoggs last night and had a look round their house. She is very clever and has done wonders without much expense. She lent me her inventory of War Department fittings, furniture, etc., of which I now attach a copy.

These little bungalows were the best accommodation available in Fayid. They were for brigadiers and major-generals.

They were all in one road, commonly known as 'Red Flannel Alley'. They were on high ground with a beautiful view of the sapphire blue Bitter Lake with the pink Sinai desert beyond. They each had a small garden which consisted of three or four inches of very fertile Nile mud spread on the hard gravel of the desert. Maxine planted a wisteria in it which climbed along the verandah at the rate of a foot a day. I planted some rose bushes, digging down through the mud into the desert to do so, and they grew like mad. We planted a clover lawn and, from the air, it was much the greenest lawn in Fayid. But that was all to come. We had not yet got the bungalow.

My letter went on:

I see no hope of any good dollop of leave this year. I am still up to my eyes in it, working seven full days a week. My only hope of any leave will be if I have to go home for conferences, and I would then try to get a week or so and fly over to Ireland.

I was up in Jerusalem about ten days ago for the last time. It was very sad and desolate.

That was five days before the British Mandate came to an end under international pressure, and our administration was withdrawing, leaving the country in a state of civil war between Jews and Arabs.

11

A Mediterranean Journey

Phoenecia Hotel, Malta, 20 May 1948:

I arrived here this evening after a good journey by BOAC Dakota from Cairo. We left Cairo at about 9.20 a.m. and flew along the North African coast. The weather was pretty good all day though hazy. But I have never seen the Mediterranean more clear. One could see the bottom a mile or more from the shore. I was puzzled by sort of false shores under the sea. There were two parallel lines of I don't know what – possibly seaweed or shells – running parallel with the shore – exactly parallel, following all the indentations, etc. There were several hundred yards of more or less sand under the sea between the real shore and the first false shore, and then an exactly similar space of clear sand between the first false shore and the second still further out to sea. I am still puzzled and would like to know the explanation. It was near Derna I saw this. I have never seen a similar formation anywhere.

We were nearly an hour at El Adem as there was rather a queue of aircraft for fuel, including our Commander-in-Chief who dropped in in his own aircraft on the way home. They no longer serve meals to passengers at El Adem at it is now only an RAF station. However General Crocker, the Commander-in-Chief, was having lunch there and said we were pretty pansy to have a BOAC lunch in the air while he had a troops' lunch on the ground!

I am staying in a palatial hotel in Malta – brand new with all modern appliances. I have a plug in the wall labelled 'Rediffusion'. I switched it on and the room was filled with the BBC – the first time I've listened to the wireless since I was at home last. The only trouble with the hotel is that water is very short. The island, which is the size of the Isle of Wight, has a population of about 350,000, and I think very little water except what is collected when it rains.

My job here has been very exacting. However, it is nearly over now and a couple of hours tomorrow will polish it off. [After a good deal of questioning, I found an officer guilty of persistent drunkenness, and suspended him from duty. He was not an MI5 officer. He was a wartime officer on secondment from the Army.] If I ever come back to Malta again, I hope it will be to do something more pleasant.

I am off next on a Mediterranean cruise! I had to go and see the C-in-C Mediterranean Fleet this morning – Admiral Sir John Power. He's a real old sea dog.

'Hello, old boy!' he said, when I walked into his room, 'haven't seen you for a long time. Where've you been stowed? Been ashore long?' (I have only met him twice before, and it was only ten days ago that I saw him.)

I explained where I'd been 'stowed', and how long I'd been 'ashore'.

'Not staying long I suppose? When are you going afloat again?'

I explained that I was aiming to go to Tripoli on Friday.

'God damn it! Friday! Going to Tripoli? How're you going?

I explained that I looked like going by RAF.

'Oh, damn the RAF! Can't go by RAF. I insist you come afloat with me. We'll stow you somewhere. I'm going to Tripoli on Friday.' (I don't know whether he was going or not, but he's going now.) 'Meet you at the Customs House steps 4.10 p.m. Flags and I'll be there and the barge will be alongside.'

He says the one thing he's revelling in in Malta is 'baccy'. (He has only recently come here.)

'Soon as I got ashore, I said to my Flag Lieutenant, "Flags

old boy! Go and buy me some baccy." He said, "Yes, sir. What sort of baccy?" "Oh, any damn baccy." Well he came back with a ruddy great tin – this size. I said to him, "Flags old boy! What are you rooking me for that? And what do you think he said? "One and eightpence." Damn it! It would have cost me a day's pay at home. Now, when anyone comes into my office, even if he has a pipe like a bucket, I throw my pouch at him and say, "Have some baccy, old boy", and when he lights his pipe, if it doesn't draw properly, I say, "Knock it out, old boy, and have another fill."'

Arthur John Power was an unforgettably attractive man. Because he was a man of exceptional character and strong personality, he was able to carry on that sort of cheerful banter with his own officers and everyone else without forfeiting one whit of his authority. And he was a splendid man with whom to do business – quick, open, intelligent, shrewd, incisive and decisive.

I met an admirer of yours today – or at least I took him to be an admirer from the way his eyes lit up when I told him you were my spouse. He is Sir David Campbell, the Lt-Governor of Malta. When we had finished our business, he said something about having been for a long time in East Africa. I mentioned that I had been down there recently. He asked me if I knew your Uncle Phil, and I told him I had been staying with him. He said he had been with him in Uganda in 1936-38, so I asked if he remembered you, which he evidently did, very vividly – but who wouldn't? He has a great regard for your uncle, but said he had always overworked in the most selfless way. He says your uncle had a rule never to work on Sundays, but he often remembers him starting on a whole night's work on Sunday night at midnight – which, of course, didn't count.

I also had a most interesting twenty minutes this morning. I had to go to see the Governor, Sir Francis Douglas. He has his office in the Palace of the Knights of Malta. I had some time to spare after seeing him, so I got one of the porters to show me round. It is a huge place, quite fascinating, and full of the most wonderful treasures. You just walk back into four and a half centuries of Europe, with pictures dating back to the sixteenth century, of popes, princes, monarchs, queens, war lords and all the rest. There are some magnificent rooms, and lovely tapestries. I wish I had had longer.

Malta is an ancient, arid, hilly island, with wonderful narrow deep water harbours, full of highly coloured fishing boats, running right into the island between the hills. Virtually all the buildings, most of them old, are built of the local stone, a soft rock of a pale cream colour which mellows in the sun to ochre. It is even more beautiful than Jerusalem because the buildings are so much older and there is also the sea. I have never seen whole masses of buildings which harmonise so well with the surrounding landscape. It would be a painter's paradise.

There are views through straight, narrow streets which are just cracks between the houses, up and down hills, to a flash of bright blue sea beyond; and many fine churches and palaces. One could spend weeks exploring the place. I, unfortunately, have only been able to snatch minutes when going on business from one place to another.

The island couldn't possibly support its population of 350,000 without the Navy, and money which comes in from other services on the sea. The people all look well and cheerful and you see no beggars or poverty. It's a real pleasure to walk through the thronging streets into which the island empties itself in the evenings. There is little traffic and the roads are filled with strolling, cheerful people.

I have been eating what I take to be Ritz-class food in this palatial hotel. It is, of course, wasted on me. I find it too rich and am replete before I have finished the soup. I prefer boiled mutton and caper sauce, but they don't have things of that sort. I have had one rather queer alimentary adventure. I had some chicken the other night for dinner. It was a very nice tender piece of chicken, and there was served with it a very white-coloured sausage which tasted familiar though I couldn't place it even with plenty of mustard which I usually find an infallible 'taster' when I am in doubt. I thought the sausage was probably made of sweetbreads or brains or something of that sort. It wasn't until I had nearly finished the course, and there was only one small piece of the sausage left, that I noticed, *mirabile dictu!*, that it was in fact a banana. Rather a curious thing, don't you think, to have with chicken? You couldn't blame someone for wondering what it was. With all due respects to the cook, I think a real sausage would have been better and less distracting and puzzling.

From Malta, 27 May 1948:

As I am sitting in the office with nothing to do while the secretaries are doing typing, etc. for me, I thought I would try to rake up a few more points of interest about Malta.

I sent a letter off this morning covered with stamps. I told the girl at the counter I wanted some nice ones and she said she had a few farthing stamps, and would I like them? I wonder if there are farthing stamps anywhere else? These colonial stamps really are great fun. I hope they will have some nice ones in Cyprus where I am aiming to go next month.

The people of Malta are obviously very much a cross between the Arabs (or rather I suppose the Berbers) and Europeans, mostly presumably Italian. The Berbers are rather different from the Arabs in that they are Hamitic, while the Arabs are Semitic. The Maltese language is also a mixture of Arabic and Italian, and I suppose older languages as well. Spoken, it sounds much more like Italian though than Arabic. Nevertheless one sees a lot of signs, etc. in the streets obviously containing words of Arabic derivation.

The people are small. I would say the average height of the men is about five foot two. Some of the younger girls are quite fetching (don't get alarmed), and the children are lovely and so animated.

The main influences in the island are the Royal Navy and the Roman Catholic Church, and they pervade everything. The former gives a pleasant and friendly atmosphere.

I am continuing this letter after lunching in the Naval Mess (ashore!). They are very nice. They all talk with exactly the same voice. I have talked over the telephone here with 'Flags' and one of the senior naval officers. They might either of them have been the Admiral's secretary in Fayid. I could tell no difference in their voices.

This business of 'ashore' and 'afloat' amuses me. One of the officers in the mess was talking to me about someone here in Malta. He said, 'I've always found him an exceedingly nice man ashore.' As I'm pretty certain that the individual has never been 'afloat' in his life, it sounded rather odd.

The Navy is the 'Grey Funnel Line', so I go by 'Grey Funnel Line' to Tripoli. I have now seen the ship. She is named the *Surprise*. One of the naval officers pointed her out to me lying in the harbour. She is a lovely-looking craft: a small naval vessel with all the part aft specially fitted up as a sort of private yacht for the C-in-C. With any luck I shall be 'stowed' aft.

Yesterday evening I was taken for a drive in the island. We went to a place called Mdina (or otherwise Notabile) which is a very ancient little walled town-cum-fortress on a hill in the middle of the island. A really fascinating place. Inside the fort there is a large church and fine old houses, in one of which the Metropolitan Archbishop of Malta lives. Others are lived in by various other Church and assorted notables; one, at least, being the present title-holder of a barony descended from one of the ancient knights. The houses have large heavy wooden doors with wonderful doorknockers. It was all very clean and quiet and dignified.

We then stood on the battlements and surveyed the island,

and watched the colours change, and mellow and fade as the sun sank. All very lovely.

We then drove to a church called the Dome. The roads are very good with stone walls along either side rather like Roscommon in Ireland except that the stone is cream-coloured. Everywhere there are lovely little shrines and churches built of cut stone. The Dome is a wonderful church. It is fairly new, and the main part of the building is a circular floor (there is no nave) surmounted by a huge dome said to be one of the largest in the world. Daylight had almost gone, and there were only a few lights burning in the church. There was insufficient light to see the many fine pictures which are built into the walls, but it was possible to get a good impression otherwise of the interior. It really is a most impressive building, all, of course, of local stone. It is exceedingly ornate, but on such a lavish and magnificent scale, of gold leaf, etc., that not only is it not vulgar, but it adds immeasurably to the glory of the scene.

But perhaps what impressed me most was a solitary praying figure. There had obviously been great ceremonies in connection with the festival of Corpus Christi during the day, and a few acolytes were clearing up the church, but over near the altar, a small figure in the open circular space of the floor, was an elderly man praying. When he had finished and got up, it was evident that he was a stonemason. He was dressed in his shabby working clothes and covered with white stone dust. (Though working clothes somehow never look shabby if they really are the clothes which share with a man his worthwhile labours.) He held his dusty cap in his hand, and his grey hair had the unaccustomed look of a man who always works with his head covered. He was a man of fifty to sixty years of age. He was so obviously a good man, and a working man, and a simple man, that there was something very impressive about him coming into the church at sundown to say his simple prayer all by himself before going home to his supper.

I understand that this fine church was built entirely by voluntary labour. The Maltese, like the Arabs of Palestine, have stone in their blood and bones. They have been working it since Neolithic times. They are undoubtedly beautiful stone workers and wonderful builders, and I am glad to see that all the new buildings now going up to replace bomb damage are being built of stone. Everywhere there are ancient quarries and not only is the stone taken out to build, but also they build into the solid rock. Quite a bit of the Naval Headquarters is underground and has been carved out of the rock.

Malta is a most charming place. There's no good comparing one place with another. You could put Malta in your pocket and drop it into a Himalayan valley and lose it, but in its own way it is as lovely a little gem as any place I have seen. Virtually all the buildings are made of the local stone which is so soft that it can be cut with a saw and an axe. They do no blasting in the quarries. It is cream-coloured when it comes out of the ground and then mellows to a tawny ochre. I did not see anyone sawing the stone, nor did I visit any quarries while they were at work, but I did see masons working on buildings cutting the stones into shape with axes.

The island being hilly and acrid, the stone buildings harmonise most beautifully with their surroundings, and usually there is a splash of the blue Mediterranean in any view. There is as much history as you could absorb in a lifetime. The history of Europe has passed through Malta in procession, leaving its mark, since the time of the Greeks; and of course, the whole place is much influenced by the history of the Knights of St John.

But I was surprised to learn that it has probably finer prehistoric remains than any other place in the world. I was told that not very long ago someone sinking a shaft through the rock came on a wonderful prehistoric temple carved out of the solid rock. I gather that it consists of a central, domed hall with other chambers leading off. It is so constructed – and they think that it would have been impossible for this to have happened accidentally – that if you whisper in a certain tone in the central hall, your voice can be heard in the other chambers as though it were a ghost speaking in your ear. The theory is that this ruse was used as a means of oracular deception.

One of the things which most struck me was the wellbeing and cheerfulness of the people.

From Tripoli, North Africa, Sunday 30 May 1948:

I was on the Customs House steps at 4.10 p.m. on Friday and 'went afloat' with the Admiral at 4.15 in the barge. We flashed across the Grand Harbour at Valetta and went aboard his private ship, the *Surprise*. She is a frigate – about 2,000 tons. She was never completed as a frigate as she was converted when new into a sort of private yacht, though she still carries some armament 'for'ard'. Aft she has a state dining room, sitting room and cabins and bathrooms. All simply but well furnished. She also has a beautiful spacious poop deck aft.

The Admiral's wife, Margaret, came afloat with us. She must be thirty years younger than he is. She was a WRNS officer whom he married last year: a very nice woman indeed, but looks very delicate. We were piped aboard with much whistling, bugles and ceremony, and I was then shown to my cabin.

'There you are, old boy! You'll be well laced in there. Stow your gear in the lockers. Tea in ten minutes. Got baccy? Flags, old boy, see the Brigadier's got plenty of baccy.'

A few minutes later the Governor of Malta, Sir Francis Douglas, and his wife were piped aboard. They were also coming on the cruise. I think he must be some high up Labour MP. A very nice, though shy and precise little man, and his wife charming. I so regaled her with Irish stories after dinner that she didn't want to go to bed. A real good solid Scots body.

At tea, the Admiral said, 'Flags, old boy, what about that poor girl who had her head cut off? When are they bringing the body on board?' This sounded a bit gruesome, but she turned up shortly afterwards – a young WRNS officer who had recently had her tonsils out and was taking ten days' leave in Tripoli. Like Charles I, she was walking and talking, if a bit hoarsely. By name Jean Strang. The rest of the party were two naval officers, Captain Gotto and Commander Pemberton. I had already been introduced to the captain of the ship, Commander Roper, and later met his First Lieutenant and the ship's doctor. I didn't get their names.

Having had tea, the Admiral suggested that we should go up on the poop deck. As we left the dining room, he said to me 'Got your pipe, old boy?'

'Yes, sir.'

'Got baccy?'

We sailed at 6 p.m. The harbour was lovely in the late evening, and all the gaily coloured little boats very pretty. There was terrific bugling and saluting as we sailed down the harbour – but no gunfire. There was an American cruiser in. Her band was lined up on deck and played 'God Save the King' as we passed her. And so out to the open sea. There was a light breeze blowing but no sea running – fortunately, as the captain of the ship told me 'She's very lively in a sea.' There was a wonderful sunset. It really got quite chilly on deck in the evening and I was glad to go below and change for dinner.

I asked Pemberton whether or not sailors got over being seasick. He said that they don't. He said that he himself is always violently sick in bad weather, even though he has had a lot of service in destroyers. However, during the war they brought out some drug for the Army when it was doing landing operations, and he says he has been taking it recently and, so long as he goes on taking the regulation doses during bad weather, he is never sick.

At dinner I sat between Gotto and the Admiral. Gotto told me that he was on the *Queen Elizabeth* the night the Italians exploded an under-water limpet mine on her hull and on the *Valiant* and a tanker in Alexandria harbour. He said that the captain of the *Valiant* was later promoted admiral and went to Italy after the Italians had joined us. He was asked one day to attend a ceremony at which Italian servicemen were being decorated. One man, due to receive the Italian VC, was the chap who had 'limpeted' the *Valiant*. When the time came, the Admiral was invited to present his decoration to him, which he did. As Gotto said, we're the only people who do such damn silly things.

For some reason I didn't sleep very well and got up in the night and looked out of the porthole. It was a lovely calm night with the moon shining across the water. By dawn we were sailing through an opal sea without a ripple except our own wake.

At 9 a.m. we passed through the breakwaters and anchored in Tripoli harbour. It is a dead harbour, full of wrecks. It is not easy to get in as there is only a narrow entrance between the remains of two ships the Germans sank to block the harbour mouth when they evacuated Tripoli.

I had a lovely day yesterday. Fortunately there is so far very little subversion in Tripoli so I have very little work to do. Today Wilfred Latham, my chap here, took me and the decapitated Wren out for a day in the country. We drove in a Jeep forty miles up the coast road towards Tunis. It is a fine road built by the Italians. We went to a place called Sabratha, which is the ruins of a Roman city. All these old places have their fascination, but this is as fine as any of them because of its lovely situation. It is built of a biscuit brown sandstone and it is right on the shore of the blue Mediterranean. It was a glorious day: bright as crystal, and the sea and the sky the most lovely colours imaginable. The sun was very strong (and I am well burnt) but there was a nice, light, fresh breeze off the sea and it wasn't hot. The ruins are most interesting, and there are a lot of mosaic floors still more or less intact. There is a very fine theatre on which the Italians did a wonderful job of restoration. They have rebuilt a lot of it using some of the original stone and a lot of new stone but of exactly the same type, and they have contrived to make something which is still a ruin; still essentially Roman; but yet sufficiently complete to give an excellent impression of the original. Sitting in the warm brown theatre looking out through the arches to the bright blue sky, and, below, the sapphire blue sea, provided an incomparably beautiful contrast of colour.

I have had a damned tough couple of years in these parts, but I know how lucky I am. It's been a very rough road, but there have been flowers by the wayside. On the whole my work has gone well and I have had great interest, made some good friends, and seen the world in a big way.

Last night I dined with Brigadier Blackley, the Chief Administrator of Tripolitania, and his wife. They have a lovely old Turkish house full of courtyards, fountains, etc.

I also met in the passage in the Administration Offices one Blackledge, who ran a garage in Athlone, and who was a very keen follower of the South Westmeath Hunt when I was Master. He's now a lieutenant-colonel.

Tripoli is a charming place. The town itself is mainly a modern Italian town. The country round about is flat with a lot of palm groves, vineyards, etc. Like all Italian places, it has excellent roads. The sun was strong, but the temperature was not high. It was perhaps just a bit hotter than fine summer weather at home. It never does get very hot along the North African coast. They don't even have fans in Tripoli. Of course you get the odd days with a south wind off the desert when it is pretty hot, but otherwise it is a good climate.

I climbed into a BOAC York plane at Castel Benito

airport, some twenty miles from Tripoli, at 4 a.m. on Tuesday morning; was in Cairo at 9 a.m., and drove straight down here and was in my office before the lunch break. A wonderful thing modern transport! – or is it? Perhaps it will kill us through forcing us to work too hard and too quickly.

12

Middle East Journey

From Baghdad, Iraq, 24 June 1948:

Here I am in Baghdad. I came by RAF Dakota. It was the usual uncomfortable RAF aircraft with just a bench down the side. There were few passengers and a lot of freight.

We flew across Sinai and the Dead Sea to Mafrak in Transjordan. The airfield at Mafrak merely consists of two landing strips marked out on the hard clay desert. No airport or anything of that sort. We got out and stood in the sun on the desert while the aircraft was refuelled from a petrol tanker. There was a strong north wind blowing, and it was reasonably cool.

We left Mafrak about noon and flew to Habbanniya which takes about two and a half hours. It was pretty bumpy all the way. One man on the aircraft was looking very green. When we landed he told me that he was very nearly sick a dozen times. He was an airman and had 3,000 flying hours and said he had never felt airsick before. It was quite cold flying and I was glad to wrap a raincoat around me.

We had some tea, and then a swim in the very nice RAF swimming bath. There were quite a few children bathing, all swimming like frogs. One little chap, who couldn't have been much more than three, was amusing himself jumping off the high diving board into the deep end. He then swam rather like a whale. He hadn't got the idea quite right. He put his head down and swam under water and every now and then lifted his head for air and then down he went again.

I spent yesterday in Habbanniya and drove up to Baghdad – some sixty miles – in the evening. I had work to do in 'Hab' concerned with the subversive threat to the territory and I lunched with the AOC, Air Vice-Marshal Grey, and his wife. He has a lovely house which they manage to keep beautifully cool.

Habbanniya was built by the RAF before the war and is an excellent station with very good buildings and amenities. The Euphrates is just next door so they have lots of water, and there are plenty of trees and grass everywhere. It is pretty warm at present in central Iraq with temperatures knocking up to 110°, but the nights cool down much more than in India. I slept outside last night. I did not need anything over me but with a comparable day temperature in India one would have needed a fan even outside to be comfortable.

I have quite a bit of work to do here and I leave on Saturday evening by the Nairn bus which takes eighteen hours to cross the desert and gets me to Damascus the next day, Sunday, morning.

The security threats to Iraq were considerable. There were the Soviet subversive and espionage threats which we had all over the Middle East, but I felt particularly nervous of the Iraqi Army which might try to seize power and which I felt that the Iraqi intelligence authorities had not got sufficiently covered. From Baghdad, 26 June 1948:

We have had a fairly strong wind and a lot of awful dust so thick that we have not seen the sun for two days. However it has brought the temperature down. I shall be glad to shake off this dust. Iraq never did attract me and I am glad I am not stationed here. The Levant and Cyprus should be a very pleasant contrast.

When I was in Baghdad, as always when I was there, I had long talks with Bhajat Beg, the Iraqi Director of Security, who became a close friend of mine. He even came to England and Maxine and I entertained him. He had, as I have already said, considerable security problems in Iraq and I emphasised my uneasiness about the Iraqi Army. He greatly liked and admired the British and much regretted the day when we ceased to administer the country

When, ten years later, in 1958, the military coup took place, in which the whole Royal Family – men, women and children – were murdered one morning, he was seized by the Army and publicly hanged. He had a young wife with whom, as he told me, he had a very intimate and affectionate relationship. The mutineers had no mercy on her. I was told later that she was taken to the scene of the execution and made to denounce her husband in public. She was then told to pull on his feet to finish him off.

I left Baghdad on the evening of 26 June 1948 by the Nairn bus. It is really a wonderful thing. It consists of a large diesel tractor coupled to a sort of pullman coach. The coach is rather like an aircraft inside, with windows opposite each row of seats. It holds seventeen passengers. It is air-conditioned and beautifully cool, the seats are very comfortable and can be let down into a reclining position for sleeping, and there is a good electric light over each seat for reading at night.

The bus and tractor together are about 75 feet long. They are very well sprung, and run on huge tyres which must be in the region of four feet high. I take it that these buses have been evolved through many years of experience of this desert route, and have been designed particularly for the job. There were two of them in our convoy. The company was started by two penniless English brothers after the First World War. They still own it, and are said now to be exceedingly wealthy.

The distance from Baghdad to Damascus is about 600 miles. Virtually the whole journey lies across the desert. There is a road the whole way across which goes to Palestine, but the Damascus route only follows this road for part of the way and then branches off northwards. In this latter part of the journey there is no road: the bus just runs on the desert. However, the going is pretty good and the bus maintains speed. I am not sure where we left the Palestine road, but I think probably just after passing Rutbah about the middle of the desert.

I very well recall the ethereal midnight atmosphere at the little pumping and refuelling halt at Rutbah. Although it was the middle of the night when we left, outside the reflected light off the wide desert all around us was so bright that, standing in the open desert, it was possible to read a newspaper. And the lifeless silence of the vast expanse of surrounding desert was broken only by the low guttural Arabic murmurings of a small group of men squatting over their hubble-bubble, and the occasional distant baying of a pi-dog.

I managed to get in five or six hours' good sleep, which says a good deal for the comfort of the bus. We had had a sort of 'cellophane' meal (and there were iced drinks also) at about 8 p.m.

It was a lovely bright starry night with a glow on the horizon caused I think by the reflection of the moonlight off the open desert. I was reminded of nights in the Lut desert in Persia. When the dawn came we were travelling over a vast, gently undulating area of fine soil. It was quite evidently only a desert through lack of water. Given water, it would be a great grain-growing country. Gradually the undulations turned to hills as we approached the Syrian mountains. The country became not unlike the plateau lands of Persia, though without such mighty mountains. At length we stopped not very far from Damascus at the customs post of Ábu-el-Shãmãt.

There we had a cup of tea in a little roadside tavern. It was a glorious champagne morning – bright and clear with a blue sky, and a sharp morning breeze blowing, so fresh after Baghdad.

After a rather long wait when the customs officer was got out of bed, we drove on into Damascus, through miles of orchards, farms and vineyards, with a view all the way of either Mount Hermon or Mount Lebanon, on which there was still snow.

Damascus itself is a very attractive town with a fairly modern air about it, set in a broad valley between the mountains, and with a river running through the middle of the town. The river is formed from the confluence of the Abana and Pharphar of the Bible which meet outside the town, but no one knows which is which. The climate is good, and Damascus, being some 3,000 feet above sea level, is not hot in the summer. I did not get time for much rubber-necking but I did have a look at the 'Street called Straight'.

David Beaumont-Nesbitt, my representative, who was also the Assistant Military Attaché in Beirut, met me in Damascus and lodged me in a comfortable hotel. My security business in Syria went off without difficulty.

Leaving Damascus we motored to Beirut. The road first leads through a valley with a joyful river running through it, and then up onto an arid undulating plateau. It then drops into a deep, broad, well-cultivated valley. It crosses the valley and then winds up to the top of the Lebanon mountains, where it was really quite cold. From there it drops down to the coast and Beirut.

It was a hair-raising journey with a lunatic driver, and a fairly strong stream of cars all driven by people who would be certifiable elsewhere.

Beirut is a lovely place. A beautiful blue Mediterranean bay surrounded by mountains. The town itself is fairly modern, built on a series of hills. It reminds one somewhat of the Italian lakes, with pretty red roofs and many flowering trees.

Again, I am in a good hotel with a view over the bay from my bedroom window, and I go to sleep to the sound of the waves washing on the rocks. I have also been bathing in the sea every afternoon. The first day it was rough and I had fun diving through the curling breakers. David Beaumont-Nesbitt has done everything to make me comfortable here, and the people I deal with are friendly and hospitable. Our Minister (Sir William Houston-Boswell) is delightful – from both business and social angles – and the best of company. He has kindly had me to lunch twice.

Beaumont-Nesbitt's office is very small – himself and two girls. As one of the girls had a birthday yesterday I took them all to dine at a local restaurant. The food was good and there was an excellent cabaret.

I really am very lucky indeed to be able to see so much of the world, and mostly in great comfort. It is all very interesting, and I get ample opportunities for meeting and picking the brains of able people who have reached the top or somewhere near it in their own sphere. I like to see how the different individuals run their own shows, and I come more and more to the conclusion that the man who can run a happy show, provided he knows his own mind and is set on reaching his objective, gets better results than the 'driver'. If people are driven they go as far as they are driven. But, if they are told what is wanted, and left to get on with it in a happy atmosphere, they go to the limit of their abilities.

Before I leave the Middle East, I am tempted to describe an 'Arabian night' on the occasion of another visit to Baghdad. Norman Himsworth, my member of our diplomatic mission there, informed me that he and I had been invited by two senior and influential local officials to dine with them, and spend the evening as their guests.

The place where they chose to entertain us was what? A night club, perhaps? I think not quite that. A restaurant? Something more than that. At all events, the food was very good of its indigenous oriental kind, and there was a continuous cabaret: act after act of multi-toned music; singing – a shade too nasal to be altogether agreeable to occidental ears –

accompanied by dextrously fingered string instruments and hand- and finger-beaten small drums; and dancing, including of course belly-dancing, but all unexceptionably seemly, given that even the most decorous of such acts are liable to have detectable (no – I did not say delectable) erotic undertones. There was no undue exposure, and nothing to which Mary Whitehouse – nor Norman nor I – could take exception; and our two local hosts were excellent conversationalists and very good company.

There was, too, the fact that the owner of the place and his lively wife, professional middle-class people, perhaps in their mid-thirties, making a hard-earned living out of this local equivalent of inn-keeping, were particularly attentive to us throughout the meal, ensuring that we wanted for nothing that they could provide. When we had finished our dinner, they invited us behind the scenes into their own private apartment for coffee, cigars and liqueurs.

We were taken into a quite spacious and comfortable sitting room where two or three of the dancing girls, now changed into normal evening frocks, were relaxing and drinking coffee. We did not sit on the floor. The room was furnished with Western-style soft furnishings, sofas and chairs, with well-chosen Persian carpets underfoot.

There was, however, one extraordinary contrasting feature to the general atmosphere of domestic comfort. On the far end of a divan sat a solitary girl who had not been performing in the cabaret. She was holding a brandy bottle by the neck and, as we came into the room, she waved it at us, shouted 'Cheerio!' and took a swig. She then slumped into the divan again. No one seemed to take any notice of her.

We were invited to be seated, and I was placed on the divan next to the brandy girl. As I sat down, she waved the bottle at me, cried out 'Cheerio!', took her swig, and drooped back again into her self-absorbed reverie.

Our hostess having, with her husband, seen to our wants, came and sat on the other side of me and we drank our coffee together. Being naturally interested to know what sort of a life these people had, I managed to get her, and later her husband, when he came and talked to me, to tell me about their business. By hard work, and hard thought, they just about managed to scrape a decent living out of it. It meant late nights always, and a short night's sleep, as they had to be in the market at dawn to get the prime fruit, vegetables, meat and fish that they needed for the restaurant. Having children, it was difficult to make up sleep even at siesta-time in the early afternoon.

Top class performers for the cabaret were essential to attract a well-heeled clientele who would spend generously. The star of that particular evening, who would be a major draw for the next fortnight, was an Egyptian dancing girl, famed throughout the Middle East. They told me what they had to pay her – somewhat more than the salary of the British Prime Minister. Her beauty was more oriental than occidental – she was a shade too plump perhaps for Western tastes – but, even to my untutored eye, she looked an exceptionally lissom, polished and delicately expressive performer, using every inch of her body, to the very tips of her fingers, to bewitch her audience; and certainly her performance brought the house down, with a chorus of cries of the equivalent of 'encore' for a repetition of her magic. In the relaxed domesticity of our hosts' sitting room, she was modesty itself, quiet and unassertive. It would have been hard to guess that she had the will and determination to put in the long and unremitting hours of practice needed to perfect her act, or that once before the footlights, she could summon up the transcendental magic which had brought her fame.

While engaged in these interesting conversations and reflections, I could not but be constantly reminded of the solitary girl beside me with the bottle of brandy, for the evening was punctuated by her spasmodic cries of 'cheerio!', accompanied each time by another swig. I tried to engage her in conversation, and would have liked to have taken the brandy bottle from her, but she would not speak to me. She seemed entirely self-absorbed.

[152]

Then I had an opportunity to ask our hostess about her. What was the matter? Why was she behaving like that? What, indeed, was she doing there?

'Oh! She's one of our dancers; not a star, but one of our own local regular girls. She's a nice girl, and well trained, and she is friendly, and the regular patrons like her. Although not brilliant, and she never will be, her pleasant personality is quite a draw.'

'But', I said, 'she wasn't performing tonight.'

'No. We couldn't let her go on tonight; she is in a very emotional state. She has just been jilted by her boyfriend and she's very upset, so she's drowning her sorrows, and we think it best to take no notice of her until she feels more composed. The brandy will put her to sleep. She is sound at heart, and she'll be back on the boards in a day or two.'

At that moment there was a crash behind me. 'Cheerio' had fallen off the divan, and the now empty brandy bottle was rolling across the carpet.

Our host and hostess jumped up and went to her, picked her up and carried her out of the room. They were gone some time, we supposed while they were putting her to bed. When they returned, they seemed rather upset, as well they might be at such an occurrence in the presence of honoured guests. So, thanking them for their hospitality, and an enjoyable and interesting evening, we took our leave, and went out into the bright moonlit night, where all was by this time quiet save for the occasional pi-dog baying the moon. And so to bed, having parted from our two distinguished local friends.

Many years later Norman asked me: 'Do you remember the evening at that oriental night club?'

'Yes, very well.'

'Do you recall the "Cheerio" girl?'

'I do indeed.'

'Do you recall that she fell off the end of the divan and had to be carried out?'

'Yes, I do.'

'Do you know what was the matter with her?'

'Yes. She had been jilted, drowned her sorrows in too much brandy, and passed out.'

'No.'

'What then?'

'She was dead.'

In the air between Cyprus and Egypt, 7 July 1948:

I left Beirut by a Cyprus Airways Dakota. The Beirut airport seemed to be run on a slap-happy basis. Some chap took my passport and said that I would get it back on the aircraft. It was not until we had taken off and were well out over the sea that the pilot discovered that the passengers had been told by the Lebanese authorities that their passports would be given to the pilot, and he had been told that they had already been returned to the passengers. So we had to go back to get them.

It was damned hot in Cyprus with the temperature up to 109°, though inland in Nicosia, which is in the middle of the island, it cools down well at night.

Cyprus is really pretty big, 140 miles long at its longest and 60 miles across at its widest. The population is 450,000. It has a large mountain feature at its southern and western end, the highest point being Mount Olympus, just over 6,000 feet. There is another fairly extensive mountain feature stretching from the centre of the northern side of the island eastwards along the 'pan-handle'. The rest of the island is a gently undulating plain, burnt as dry at this time of year as the Punjab.

I had to go and see the Governor, Lord Winster, who had just moved up to his summer place in the hills at Troodos near Mount Olympus. The hills are very like the foothills of the Himalayas, but lack the exotic cactus, etc. and the trees are not comparable to the great deodars. However, there are lots of cedars and pines and it is cool and pleasant. The

Governor's House (officially called 'The Governor's Cottage') is a small English country house, with a delightful little garden, and surrounded by large pine trees. We arrived about noon and stayed to lunch. I liked Lord Winster very much, and his wife. They are neither of them young, and I should have put them at beyond the normal retiring age.

We returned to Nicosia by another road, so I managed to see a good bit of the island. Cyprus is threatened both by Soviet and Greek subversion, so I was busy.

The fact that that letter was written in the air between Cyprus and Egypt prompts me to tell of another flight later on, after Maxine and the family had joined me in Egypt.

I left Fayid early one morning in an RAF Anson to fly to Nicosia. I had some very urgent business to do, concerning the misconduct of an officer. I think I was the only passenger in the little twin-engined plane. The distance we had to fly is 350 miles. When, by my watch, we had gone nearly half-way, the pilot banked and went into an 180° turn and headed south again towards Egypt. I was sitting over the port wing and, looking out of the window, I saw that the engine below me was on fire and pouring smoke. The flames were coming in flashes, but the smoke was continuous. The engine was still running, and the wing itself had not caught fire.

I realised that the pilot could not see what was going on. He only had his instruments to tell him that something was amiss. It seemed to me that if he kept the engine running, fuel must be being pumped into it; that would feed the flames, and the wing might catch fire; so I went and had a word with him. I told him what I could see, and suggested that, if the Anson could fly on one engine, it might be safer if he stopped the other one. He said he could fly on one engine, losing height progressively, but he would have to give the aircraft so much rudder that his leg would not stand the strain long enough to get us back to Egypt, and he would rather try to make land than 'ditch' in the sea.

I can imagine – indeed, I prefer not to imagine – events in the air that must be terrifying. This one was not like that. It was slow-moving and, curiously, not frightening. Rather it was an unusual and interesting situation. The fire seemed well contained in the engine and did not get worse. My role was not wholly passive. I had the self-appointed job of keeping an eye on the engine and letting the pilot know of any significant change. As we were losing height, I thought it likely that we would have to ditch, but that did not seem very desperate either. It was a brilliant fine day; it was still early morning, so there were many hours of daylight ahead. The approaches to the Suez Canal north of Egypt are full of shipping. The pilot ought to be able to put down near a ship; if not, he could certainly make our exact position known, so there should be no great trouble in finding us and picking us up. I suppose we carried some life-saving equipment, but I do not recall that we did anything about it. The Anson has a low stalling speed; the pilot was a cool customer, and I supposed competent, and I therefore thought that he would do an efficient ditching operation. I reckoned that, at the worst, if we had nothing to hang on to, I could float for hours in the warm sea – so I sat back and kept a careful watch, ready to take any immediate appropriate action that might be necessary.

In the event we made land. We came fairly low over the Egyptian coast, and there were a number of airfields between us and Fayid on which we could land. But the pilot was determined to make base if he could, so we flew down the Suez Canal leaving a trail of smoke, and just made the Fayid airfield by flying straight in instead of the preliminary circling which was customary in those days. We were escorted up the runway by a convoy of fire engines and ambulances.

There was a little coffee bar on the airfield, and I went in there for a cup while waiting for a motor-car from Headquarters. The pilot came in and had a cup with me. He said that a locking nut had broken on one of the cylinders of the engine; the ring holding the cylinder head to the cylinder block had therefore come loose; the piston had then gone through the cylinder head so every time the cylinder fired it shot out a flash of flame and smoke.

He said that when he had got to the airfield that morning he had turned down all four Ansons that he had been offered as he had some doubts about the airworthiness of all of them. However, he was told that he must take one as there was a passenger with an urgent need to get to Cyprus. That was me.

It was shortly after the Second World War and the aircraft in which we flew all over the Middle East and East Africa were old and well worn. They were, however, well maintained by the RAF, who had a rule which added to their potential passengers' confidence in them. The engineers engaged on an overhaul job had to go up in the aircraft the first time it flew after the overhaul. That must, in Dr Johnson's words, 'have concentrated their minds wonderfully'.

Late that evening I was told that something would fly to Cyprus next day, so the early morning again found me waiting in the little coffee bar. The same pilot came in

'We're off,' he said.

'In what?' I asked.

'The same kite as yesterday. They've fitted a new engine.'

The best of a not very good lot again, I thought, as I climbed aboard muttering, '*Om Mane Padme Hum*', the Tibetan supplicatory mantra.

We reached Nicosia safely, where I had to face the ugly situation, hardly more agreeable than being in a burning aeroplane, of dealing with the alleged misconduct of our representative there. He was another wartime Army officer, not an MI5 officer. We returned him to the Army.

Maxine was by chance involved in this matter. She has given me the following account of her involvement:

When I arrived at Fayid in the Canal Zone with our boys to join Bill, it was a pleasure to find that Mollie and Goff Hamilton were also stationed there. I had known Mollie since the days when she and I had spent our school holidays

[157]

with Aunt Bee, the dear old martinet who used to care for children whose parents were abroad. I well remembered the beautiful cards and calendars painted by Mollie and others later reproduced by the Medici Society, received annually by Aunt Bee.

Mollie and Goff were struggling at that time to maintain themselves and their two daughters on a major's pay from which Goff also had to pay alimony to his first wife in Ireland. This was very hard going and Mollie (who later became well known as the author M. M. Kaye) suggested that we might make a joint trip to Cyprus to paint in that beautiful island, and have an exhibition on our return, which would hopefully help the Hamilton finances.

So we set off. We took passages on the deck of a Greek boat – for cheapness, with our neighbours of many nationalities being sick on the deck all around us. A very disagreeable experience. We were met at Limassol by Bill's 'man in Cyprus' – let us call him Bullock. He was sweating, shaking and highly nervous. I knew I was the wife of the boss but was astonished that I appeared to cause this reaction.

He drove us across the island to Nicosia in a most reckless fashion. Mollie said if she had not still felt so seasick she would have died of fright. When we reached his office he asked for a private word with me – and took me behind the building. He then told me that his wife had just run off with a Greek doctor, and he was distraught. I felt most concerned for him, pressed his hand and said I quite understood his upset feelings, which in my mind must have accounted for his reckless driving, and arranged to leave with Mollie as soon as we could in our small hired car.

Our destination was a house in Kyrenia run as a guest house by Mrs Worcester – known as 'Mrs Wu'. Her husband had made a fortune in Shanghai and had left in a hurry with all his household treasures. He had stopped off in Cyprus where he had died, leaving Mrs Wu ensconced amongst the most fabulous Chinese treasures, jade screens and figures and vast oriental jars, at one time visited by King Farouk of Egypt to take the pick of her collection. The treasures had gradually become covered in dust and hung with cobwebs and Mrs Wu was reduced to taking paying guests.

The morning after our arrival a visitor was announced. This was 'Mrs Bullock', who informed me that her husband had been carrying on with his secretary to such a degree that she, Mrs Bullock, had been forced to leave and to fly into the arms of a Greek doctor. What else could she do? The day after her visit Bullock called, in a very emotional state. He went down on one knee to assure me that he and his secretary were soul-mates and attended communion together. Mollie suspected he might try to do me harm and kept popping round the jade screen asking me if she could 'borrow my bunjy'.

After his departure I decided to send Bill a telegram to ask him to sort out his Cyprus office. I did not know that the Governor had also done so. This was soon followed by a telephone call from Bullock – furious that Bill was coming – and followed rapidly by another call to say that Bill's aircraft was on fire over the Mediterranean. Mollie rang Bullock to ask where the call had come from. He replied to the effect that he neither knew nor cared, and Mollie came back to me to say that all was well as Bill had got back to Egypt – quite untrue. She spent the rest of the day in acute anxiety as every aircraft she heard she feared was searching for Bill in the Mediterranean.

Bill finally arrived in the same ropy aircraft that had been on fire, and was treated to the same terror-driving tactics by Bullock. It would have taken more than that to frighten off Bill, who firmly settled the Bullock drama. Mollie's imagination had been fired – she had just started to write crime novels. She said to me 'What would the Secret Service do now?' I replied that no one in it would say, and no one else knew, so she could invent what she liked. Mollie then turned it into a gun-running novel, in which I am pushed off the top of St Hilarion. I am fortunately saved by my long hair catching in a bush, from where I am rescued by Bill! It all appears in *Death in Cyprus*, one of M. M. Kaye's series of thrillers.

13

Reunion; and Vale to the Indian Army

Much of my correspondence with Maxine during the next two months related to our forthcoming accommodation in Fayid, but there were other topics. From Cairo, 18 July 1948:

I have had a pretty hectic week and had to dash off to Amman, the capital of Transjordan, in a hurry.

Amman is full of Arab refugees from Palestine. [A million of them had been driven out of Palestine by the Jews and were a considerable political security problem.] Some genuine poor people; others, rich Arabs. Amman is a very ancient place. It was Philadelphia, one of the cities of the Decapolis. It is quite a small town built of stone in and on the hillsides of a rocky ravine. It is over 2,000 feet up and, though hottish in the day, is beautifully cool at night. The only really interesting thing I came across this time – apart from my legitimate business – was the place where Uriah the Hittite was slain 'in the forefront of the battle'. A typical sordid, immoral, cruel, deceitful tale. The site of his death is not historical tradition, but is arrived at by deduction, as the ground admitted of only one course of action in the battle and the place can be accurately deduced to within a few square yards.

There was no RAF plane going through from Mafrak to Fayid for another three days, and no RAF plane in Amman which could take me back, so I came down to Cairo today on an Egyptian Airlines plane. It was a beautiful day with good visibility up to 100 miles or so and I could see most of

Palestine. There was a big fire – or at least a lot of smoke – coming from the area of the north wall of the old city of Jerusalem. That is the area of the Damascus Gate, where most of the fighting has been going on during the last few days. It seemed to me that we were flying stupidly near to Jewish-held parts of Palestine, particularly as our aircraft was only an ancient Rapide biplane with a top speed of 120 m.p.h. and covered in Egyptian markings, and the Jews are believed to have modern fighters. However, we were not disturbed.

When we landed, I asked the Egyptian pilot why he didn't take a safer course by cutting southwards round the south end of the Dead Sea. He said, 'Not to worry! If I go that way I go short of petrol for reaching Cairo. If I go my way I may meet Jewish.' I said, 'I'd prefer to go short of petrol and land at Ismailia and get some more, than get shot full of holes by Jewish.' He thought that quite funny.

From Fayid, Egypt, 19 September 1948:

I reached Cairo (from London) yesterday evening, and motored down here this morning – Sunday.

This is the season of the sirocco winds and of thunderstorms in the Mediterranean. We flew through a bit of a wonderful storm just off the south west tip of Sicily. It was late in the evening and the sun was low. Great pillars of snow-white cloud stood up from a real inferno where clouds like tongues of flame licked upwards from huge smoking grottoes. It was just the ancients' idea of Hell. When we were through the storm, I looked back. The sun was now behind it, and the cloud seemed like a blood-red curtain in the sky.

It then got dark and we flew in the moonlight. One of those pictures which I think will remain photographed on my mind is of the islands at Malta appearing, as I looked forward over the wing, like black shadows on the moonlit sea.

Perhaps I may add one more flying tale. I once had to make a flight in a light aircraft across the Borneo jungles. The aircraft took only three people, the pilot and one passenger who sat beside him, and a second passenger seated behind them. There was on my flight another passenger, a senior police officer, who admitted that he disliked flying and always felt nervous. His condition was not improved by the briefing we got from the pilot before we boarded the aircraft. He said: 'It is not possible to land anywhere between here and our destination as it is thick forest all the way. I must therefore show you what to do in case we have to come down in the forest and I am killed. We have a fortnight's survival kit and rations on board. We also have various tools including an axe, and flares and other things. Now, I'll show you where they're stowed.'

There were squally rain showers about, and he added: 'I hope the weather doesn't get any thicker because it makes navigation difficult. There are no navigation aids, and I have to navigate by hills and large and distinctive trees that I recognise and, of course, by my compass.'

After that, the other unfortunate passenger was knocking at the knees as we climbed aboard. To get the trim of the aircraft right, he sat behind, and I sat beside the pilot. The engine started up – 'chocks away', and we were off. We dodged round the rainstorms for half-an-hour or so, then, as it was too noisy for conversation, the pilot reached down and pulled out a notepad and wrote something on it. I read it, and handed it back to the other passenger. A look of horror came over his face. He assumed it would be saying, 'We're conking out and coming down in the jungle'; but in fact it said, 'We're doing fine. Should be there in twenty minutes.'

I wrote, on 25 September 1948, to Maxine: 'The accommodation is now fixed. I am just longing to have you all with me and I am sure you will get a great welcome from many nice and kind people here.'

I hoped that, if her ship berthed for any length of time at Piraeus, Maxine might get a chance to visit Athens. I quite often had to go there and, in those years, just after the Second

World War, it was quite a small old city, and there were no tourists. I recall in particular the occasion when, in the evening, after a hot summer's day, I climbed the Acropolis. There was no one there. I had the whole place to myself, and I sat on the warm marble steps of the Parthenon and watched the sun set over the Bay of Salamis, and I lived that moment alone with 3,000 years of time and history.

I engaged some Sudanese servants, who proved excellent. They were also given to having ingenious ideas of their own to lighten our lives. For instance, at Christmas they thought the brandy butter rather dull so they coloured it with cochineal. We always gave a large Christmas party for my officers and secretaries, and we had to have two turkeys. To brighten up the turkeys the Sudanese put an electric torch, covered in red paper, inside each to shine out through their rear ends.

Maxine and I had been married for eight years but the exigencies of war and post-war conditions had been such that not only had we had an enormous amount of separation, but also our little bungalow in Fayid was the first home of our own that we had had since our first few weeks of married life in our tented home in Delhi.

While this was the beginning of a new family life for us, it was also the end of an old life for me. In August 1947 Independence – and Partition – came to India. This involved the fading out of the British officers in the Indian Army, and I resigned my commission. My resignation took effect from 30 August 1948, a few weeks before Maxine and the boys joined me in Egypt, but MI5 asked me to remain on in my appointment in Egypt, which I did for the next two and a half years until 1951.

Some time after I had left the Middle East things gradually came to a head everywhere. The Middle East fell apart by degrees. Civil war in Greece and the flight of the Royal Family. The serious EOKA rebellion in Cyprus. Civil war in Palestine. Civil war and anarchy in the Lebanon. Military coup in Iraq and slaughter of the whole Royal Family. Assassination of the ruler of Jordan (formerly Transjordan). Political takeover and dismissal of the Royal Family in Egypt. Violent clerical takeover and dismissal of the Royal Family in Persia. A series of coups and final military takeover in Syria. And in East Africa armed civil strife in Somaliland and Somalia. Civil war in the Sudan. The Mau Mau in Kenya. The Aden Colony and Aden Protectorate lapsed into anarchy. It was no wonder that I had been busy in SIME with all that impending and hanging over me.

After my twenty years in the Indian Army I had two subsequent careers, each of which lasted twenty years; but they belong to the world of today and not, like my Indian Army life, to the 'days that are gone'.

If I had to start my life again, I would be a soldier (or a member of one of the other armed services). I like 'belonging', and there is no more agreeable, and no more useful, life. The armed forces provide the shield behind which the community at large can carry on its life in peace and security. Pacifism and conscientious objection are a cop-out from reality unless one takes the absurd view that a nation should not defend itself, or that the 'dirty work' should be left to others – a 'holier than thou' attitude. I once asked Bryan Emery, the Egyptologist, whether there was any common factor in the downfall of the various ancient Egyptian dynasties. 'Yes,' he replied. 'A community is in decline when the sons of its leading families no longer join the armed forces.'

And one other thing I would do if she would have me. I would think myself more than fortunate to marry the same wife again. She has striking talents and qualities which this book does not adequately reveal; but that is another story which deserves to be told.

At all events I cannot be accused of a lack of constancy.

When I was perhaps three-quarters of the way through this book, I said to Maxine that writing it was making me feel sad. Reliving the fun and the friendships, the work and the play, that had been our lives all those years ago brought me forcibly up against the reality that so many of those we had known so well are no longer with us. Being an old Persian hand, lines of *Omar Kháyyám* were often in my mind:

> Lo! Some we loved, the loveliest and the best
> That Time and Fate of all their vintage prest,
> Have drunk their cup a round or two before,
> And one by one crept silently to rest.

When my time was up in SIME in 1951, MI5 offered me a permanent place on their staff. I went home to their headquarters in London and was one of the directors of MI5 for fifteen years until I reached retirement age. I was for many years director of the overseas department, E Branch. I had to advise all the Commonwealth countries, and to liaise with friendly foreign countries, all of which involved a great deal more travelling. I also at one time directed F Branch, the counter-subversion branch, and for a time C Branch, the practical security branch.

When I directed the overseas department I was personally involved on the ground in all the disturbances and violence associated with the dissolution of Empire: the Communist revolt in Malaya, the Mau Mau uprising in Kenya, the EOKA campaign in Cyprus, the uprising in Aden, the Indonesian assault on Borneo.

I was forever grateful to have had the chance to work with such able and professional people as the colleagues whom I had in MI5. Nothing can give more satisfaction than to be privileged to work among the 1st XI, and both men and women were as nice as they were competent.

In SIME Maxine took great care to look after the girls and families in the office, and continued to do so at home for office wives and families. She has been made an honorary member of the MI5 pensioners' association, which meets for a lunch twice a year when the Director-General gives us a talk to bring us up to date on what the service is doing.

In the next twenty years of my life I had a quite exceptionally interesting time running with Maxine the successful international business which she started. I retired from that at the age of eighty, since when I have painted and sold many pictures in aid of charity, kept active around the house, and written several books.

I have been fortunate in the life I have had – an ideal marriage, plenty of adventure, and much solid worthwhile work shared with devoted colleagues for the defence of the Realm.

Maps

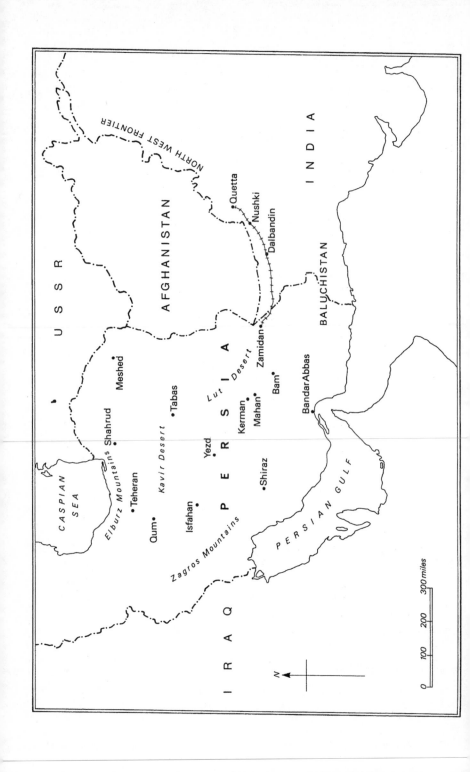

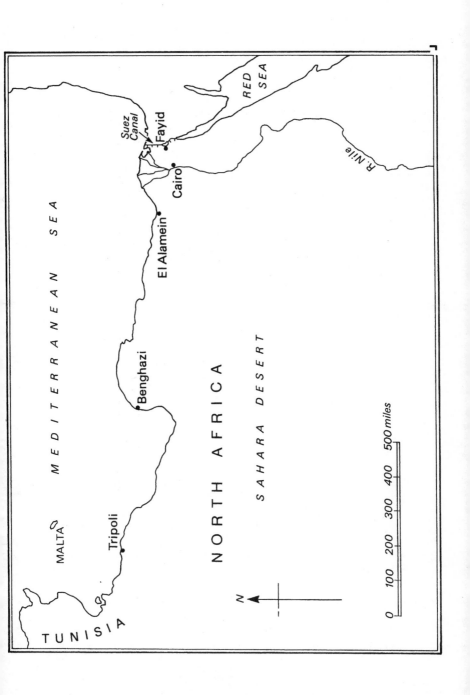

The Horn of Africa 1939

RED SEA

ARABIAN PENINSULA

Asmara

ERITREA

Kamaran Island

Perim

Aden

FRENCH SOMALILAND

Hargeisa

BRITISH SOMALILAND

ABYSSINIA

ITALIAN SOMALILAND

Mogadishu

INDIAN OCEAN

0 100 200 300 miles

N

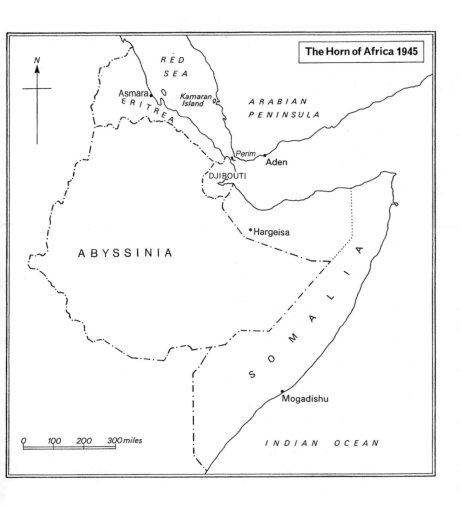

The Horn of Africa 1945

RED SEA

Asmara

ERITREA

Kamaran Island

ARABIAN PENINSULA

Perim

Aden

DJIBOUTI

Hargeisa

ABYSSINIA

SOMALIA

Mogadishu

0   100   200   300 miles

INDIAN OCEAN

Index